speaking for Ourselves

Speaking for Ourselves

Autobiographical Sketches by Notable
Authors of Books for Young Adults

Compiled and Edited by
Donald R. Gallo
Central Connecticut State University

National Council of Teachers of English
1111 Kenyon Road, Urbana, Illinois 61801

NCTE Editorial Board: Richard Abrahamson, Celia Genishi, Richard Lloyd-Jones, Raymond Rodrigues, Brooke Workman; Charles Suhor, *chair,* ex officio; Michael Spooner, ex officio

Book Design: Doug Burnett

Staff Editor: Tim Bryant

NCTE Stock Number 46252-3020

Library of Congress Cataloging-in-Publication Data
Speaking for ourselves : autobiographical sketches by notable authors
  of books for young adults / compiled and edited by Donald R. Gallo.
     p.   cm.
     Includes bibliographical references.
     Summary: Eighty-seven well-known American and English authors
  describe their life and work.
     ISBN 0-8141-4625-2
     1. Authors, American—20th century—Biography—Dictionaries.
  2. Authors, English—20th century—Biography—Dictionaries.
  3. Young adult literature, American—Bio-bibliography.   4. Young
  adult literature, English—Bio-bibliography.   5. Young adult
  literature—Authorship.   [1. Authors,American.
  2. Authors,English.]   I. Gallo, Donald R.
  PS129.S64   1990
  810.9'0054—dc20
  [B]
  [920]   89-48918
                                                                        CIP
                                                                        AC

For Margaret Early
whose faith in me and whose indefatigable example
led me into this publishing business
and
for all of my colleagues in the field of
books for teenagers
especially those who have most informed
and inspired me:

Dick Abrahamson

Bruce Appleby

Ken Donelson

Ted Hipple

Maia Mertz

Bob Probst

Bobbi Samuels

Bob Small

Anne Webb

Jerry Weiss

Contents

Acknowledgments

Because the concept for this book began with a challenge from John Lansingh Bennett when he was senior editor for publications at NCTE in 1987, thanks must go to him above everyone else. Without John's thoughtful prodding, this book never would have been conceived.

The next thank-you must go to Richard Peck, who helped me refine my goals for the collection and who suggested that instead of having a committee write biographies of authors, I ask the authors to write their own biographical sketches in order to capture each author's own voice and style.

Thanks to Richard Peck also, and to Jane Yolen, for writing the first autobiographical sketches for me to use as models for the other authors. Their support of this project no doubt encouraged other writers to contribute to this volume.

To Michael Spooner I give thanks for his encouraging comments, gracious guidance, and conscientious administration during the publishing process.

A special thanks to the many editors, publicity directors, and marketing people at all the publishing companies who provided me with addresses and contacts with their authors.

Above all, an enormous bundle of thanks goes to all the authors who wrote for this collection original, personal glimpses of their lives and influences, without thought of remuneration. This is, indeed, their book in their own words.

Introduction

How did Richard Peck get started as a writer? What motivated Anne McCaffrey to write science fiction? How has M. E. Kerr's writing been influenced by her mother? How is Sue Ellen Bridgers' life reflected in the settings of her novels? Was Paul Zindel's teenage life as bizarre as the lives of the teenage characters in his novels?

English and reading teachers in middle, junior, and senior high schools often want to know more about an author than what is provided in the very brief blurb on the dust jacket of a book. Students sometimes want to find biographical information for a report on an author. But most of the traditional sources of author biographies— e.g., *Contemporary Authors*—include information on only the most well-known authors and understandably may not include biographies of many contemporary authors who write mainly for teenage readers. Moreover, most biographical sources such as *Something About the Author* are bound in expensive, oversized hardcover editions that are available only in libraries.

This collection is an effort to provide both students and teachers with an inexpensive, readable, and convenient-size collection of information about the most notable authors of books for young adults that can be kept in the classroom or used at home for easy reference. This collection no doubt will also be of use to librarians who have an interest in young adult fiction.

Selection of Authors

By using publishers' catalogs, recent issues of *Books for You* and *Your Reading*, adolescent literature texts such as *Literature for Today's Young Adults* by Ken Donelson and Alleen Nilsen, and my own professional experience, I compiled a list of 169 names of contemporary authors— most of them American, a few Canadian and British—whose novels are popular among American teenagers. I sent an alphabetical list of those names to the forty-one past and present officers of the Assembly on Literature for Adolescents of NCTE (ALAN) asking them to identify those writers whose biographies should definitely be included in a book like this, and those who should probably be included if there is room.

From the responses of the thirty-three people—eighty percent—who returned the list, I established a ranking from the most frequently noted authors (S. E. Hinton and Paul Zindel) to the least frequently noted ones. (For a more detailed description of the process, see "Who Are the Most Important YA Authors?" in *The ALAN Review,* Spring 1989, pp. 18–20.) Each of the one hundred most noted authors was invited to write an autobiography of between four hundred and five hundred words and to provide a photograph, along with a list of their major publications. Thus, in addition to having accurate, up-to-date information, readers of this volume also have a sample of each author's style and personal voice.

Several authors responded immediately and with enthusiasm. "Thanks for including me"; "I am flattered to be considered among the most important authors of novels for young adults," they wrote. Some individuals did not respond at all, even after a second and a third request. A few others expressed clear opposition: "I don't do stuff like that," one wrote. "I'd prefer to let my books speak for themselves," another replied. One declared that she was much too busy to take the time for something like this. Still another said he would take time to write something only if he was paid $150. In the end, eighty-seven of the one hundred invited authors wrote something for this book.

To all those authors who did submit their autobiographical sketches and bibliographies, we owe great thanks. These unique sketches provide students, teachers, and librarians with lively information about our favorite authors while also introducing us to many other writers whose novels provide worthwhile and stimulating reading.

Observations

In addition to reading about individual authors, some readers may be interested in what many of these writers have in common. From among the biographical facts and helpful advice provided throughout these sketches, several interesting patterns emerge:

An abnormally large number of these writers were born in New York City. Twenty percent of them, in fact, including Avi, Paula Fox, Harry Mazer, Norma Fox Mazer, Kin Platt, Jane Yolen, and Paul Zindel.

Two others—Susan Beth Pfeffer and Todd Strasser—were born and raised on Long Island, while several more, such as Judy Blume, grew up in nearby New Jersey. Several others, born elsewhere, grew up in New York City, all of them Black: Alice Childress, Rosa Guy, Sharon Bell Mathis, and Walter Dean Myers. Some, like Norma Klein and Nicholasa Mohr, stayed in the city; others, like the Collier brothers and Gloria Miklowitz, moved elsewhere. Thus, nearly thirty percent have their roots in or around New York City.

The characteristic most common to these famous writers is their love of reading: "I started to read at four and never stopped" (H. M. Hoover). "I fell in love with books" (Robbie Branscum). "I read everything I could get my hands on" (Zilpha Keatley Snyder). Some, like Joan Aiken, were lonely, solitary children who used reading as a way into worlds more exciting than their own. "I was a bookworm and a dreamer," says Lois Duncan. "I was an only child, a reader, and a listener," writes Eve Bunting.

Listening and observing provided a foundation for a writing profession for many. Norma Fox Mazer says it best when she recalls a scene in her life at the age of thirteen: "I'm at an adult gathering, sitting well back in a big side-winged chair, feeling hidden, unseen, almost invisible. My favorite state. I can watch, think, observe."

Several writers grew up in families where storytelling and gossip flourished. Thus, for people like Isabelle Holland, Virginia Hamilton, M. E. Kerr, and Jane Yolen, storytelling was part of their heritage.

Along with listening and observing, many of these writers— including Sandy Asher, Judy Blume, Lynn Hall, Myron Levoy, Gloria Miklowitz, and Zilpha Keatley Snyder—recall a very active fantasy life as a child. And Bruce Brooks combined his love of reading with his own imagination by "making things up in words, alternative stories that went along with the ones I was reading."

Some of these writers grew up in very secure extended families, as Sue Ellen Bridgers, Jean Craighead George, Nicole St. John, and Cynthia Voigt did. Others, like Robin McKinley, Scott O'Dell, and Rosemary Sutcliff, were uprooted several times throughout their childhoods. But no one moved more than Paula Fox, who says she "attended nine schools before I was twelve."

Many started their writing careers early, immediately after school, or while still in school. Lois Duncan and Isabelle Holland sold their first stories at thirteen; Maureen Daly published her first story at fifteen. S. E. Hinton started writing *The Outsiders* at fifteen and published it at seventeen. Gordon Korman wrote his first novel in the seventh grade, earning only a B+ in English that year, and published five novels before he graduated from high school. Other noted novelists came to the field at a much later age: Richard Peck at thirty-seven; T. Ernesto Bethancourt at forty-one; and Ouida Sebestyen in her fifties after receiving hundreds of rejection slips.

One of the most evident similarities among these authors is their early knowledge of what they wanted to be when they grew up. Katie Letcher Lyle, Anne McCaffrey, Robin McKinley, Scott O'Dell, and Sandra Scoppettone, among others, all note that they had wanted to be a writer from their earliest memories. "I wanted to be a writer all my life," says M. E. Kerr. "I've known since second grade that I wanted to be a writer," notes Paula Danziger. And Lois Duncan writes, "I can't remember a time when I didn't think of myself as a writer." Vera Cleaver adds an important note to a similar statement: "Most of us . . . do know at a very early age . . . that we will spend all of our lives at writing. We also know, or we find out, that we must apprentice for the job."

Several of these novelists, such as Ellen Conford, Susan Cooper, and Myron Levoy, worked on or wrote for their high school newspapers. And as adults a large number of them worked in some aspect of the publishing business, usually in newspapers or magazines, before turning to writing novels themselves. Among them are Joan Aiken, Lloyd Alexander, James Lincoln Collier, Susan Cooper, Robert Cormier, Jean Craighead George, Constance Greene, John Rowe Townsend, and Jane Yolen. Some, like Nat Hentoff and Robert Lipsyte, remain in the mass media business while occasionally writing fiction.

A large number of authors were—and a few still are—teachers, including Robin Brancato, Christopher Collier, Paula Danziger, Paula Fox, Barbara Girion, Lee Bennett Hopkins, both of the Hadley Irwin duo, Katie Letcher Lyle, Kevin Major, Joan Lowery Nixon, Joyce Carol Thomas, Julian Thompson, and Cynthia Voigt.

A few have had other careers before and while writing novels for young adults: William Sleator was a rehearsal pianist for the Boston Ballet; both Nicholasa Mohr and Rosemary Sutcliff were visual artists; Kin Platt was a caricaturist and cartoonist.

Some of these authors—such as Paula Danziger and S. E. Hinton—have published young adult novels exclusively. Others have published in a variety of genres: short stories, poems, magazine articles, advertising copy, scholarly works, adult mysteries, plays for radio and the stage, and scripts for television and movies.

Although few writers describe their writing schedules or explain where their ideas come from, those who have, like Ellen Conford, indicate that a lot of their ideas "just happen." The characters often seem to come alive out of nowhere. The real work comes, as Virginia Hamilton asserts, in the rewriting stage, where the real creativity takes place as the writer molds and polishes the story like a sculptor working with clay. For someone like Avi, that may mean as many as thirty rewrites.

Most writers do not mention their mode of recording and revising their stories, but approximately thirty percent of the autobiographies that I received appear to have been printed by means of computer word processors. Only two were handwritten.

All of the authors appear to find great satisfaction in their profession. All of them sound dedicated to writing books that will, in some way, help kids to grow up. As Harry Mazer says, "I write my stories with the hope that they have something to say to young readers about the qualities needed to live today—indeed, to live in any time."

And all seem to work diligently at what they do, though several note that writing isn't as easy as many people imagine it to be. S. E. Hinton says, "It's hard enough even if you like to." Nevertheless, these authors find joy as well as satisfaction in their work. "Writing is the most rewarding career I can imagine," asserts Constance Greene. And Gloria Miklowitz concludes, "I can't imagine a happier way to live."

The authors have other things to say. Let them speak to you for themselves.

Joan Aiken

PHOTO: TONY WHITCOMB

A lthough my father (the poet Conrad Aiken) was American, I grew up in England, because he had moved there from Cape Cod a few years before my birth, as he thought the education would be better for my two elder siblings, John and Jane. I was never registered American, so grew up a British citizen. I was born in 1924 in a very beautiful old house, built in 1651, in the town of Rye, about eight houses along from where Henry James had lived less than ten years before. My parents were divorced when I was about four; my Canadian mother then married an English writer, Martin Armstrong, and moved to the other end of Sussex. Along with a younger half-brother, David, we lived with my stepfather in a small ancient cottage in a very small remote village, without electricity or piped water. Reading books and going for walks were our main occupations. My mother, who had degrees from McGill and Radcliffe, taught me herself till I was twelve. So I had a lonely childhood, feeling somewhat separated from the other children in the village. We had masses of books in the house, as my elder siblings had collected a great many (lots of them American); reading aloud was a great family habit—we all read to each other. We'd go for picnics on the Sussex downs, nearby, and take books to read aloud; or have silent "reading teas," where everyone was allowed to bring a book to table.

When I went to boarding school at twelve it was a shock. I stopped growing and remained at five feet. I knew far more than the rest of my class in some ways, and far less in others. I knew nothing about games, dancing, gymnastics, and just the ordinary things that children pick up at school. I was desperately shy and homesick. Going into a room full of people has been difficult ever since. But Wychwood School for Girls was actually a pleasant school, and in time I was quite happy there, though I always felt that school life was very bleak and uncivilised compared with home, where everybody was quiet, friendly, and considerate. But there were plenty of things I enjoyed: English classes, wonderful drawing classes with an inspired teacher, Marion Richardson, and later being allowed to wander about the beautiful town of Oxford. I always knew I wanted to be a writer (after all, both my father and step-father did nothing else) and began submitting poems for the school magazine. Hardly a term passed when I didn't have something in.

By the time I left school, World War II had begun; it was 1941. I knew I didn't want to go to college, and I'd had as much as I could take of living with a lot of other people in a big institution, so I took a war job with the British Broadcasting Corporation, where I was set to work filing Spanish and Portuguese correspondence. It was a dull task, so I left and took secretarial training, then landed a much more interesting job in the library of the small United Nations Information Centre, which had just been set up in London. There I met and married the press officer, Ronald Brown, and after a few years had two children.

Unfortunately, when the children, John and Liz, were five and two, their father died and I had to go back to work, editing other people's stories for *Argosy* magazine (which had taken a few of my stories). I had gone on writing in my spare time all this while, switching from poetry to short stories. By now I'd had two books of children's short stories published and a juvenile novel, which I had written at age seventeen and now revised. I left *Argosy* and did a short spell writing advertising copy at the London office of J. Walter Thompson, then decided to chance becoming a full-time freelance. The first thing I did was to finish a book I'd started at the time when my husband fell ill and I'd had to abandon; I'd always had it at the back of my mind. It was *The Wolves of Willoughby Chase*, which, when it came out in the United States, did very well and justified my rash plunge into full-time writing. (It has just been made into a film.)

After that, life was really just writing and more writing. I now divide my time between England and America; I remarried ten years ago, and my present husband is Julius Goldstein, a New Yorker who teaches at CUNY. By now the total of my books is somewhere in the eighties (I write novels for adults, too). My favourite kind of writing is still the fantasy short story. Novels have to be carefully planned, television work is full of rules, plays need an immense amount of thought and technique. But short stories . . . they come closest to free flight.

Bibliography

Books for Young Adults (selected)

1960	*The Kingdom and the Cave*
1962	*The Wolves of Willoughby Chase*
1964	*Black Hearts in Battersea*
1966	*Night Birds on Nantucket*
1968	*The Whispering Mountain*
1969	*Night Fall*
1971	*The Cuckoo Tree*
1974	*Midnight Is a Place*
1977	*Go Saddle the Sea*
1981	*The Stolen Lake*
1983	*Bridle the Wind*
1986	*Dido and Pa*
1987	*The Moon's Revenge*
1988	*The Teeth of the Gale*

Short Story Collections (selected)

1968	*A Necklace of Raindrops*
1971	*The Kingdom Under the Sea* (folktales)
1974	*Tales of Arabel's Raven* (in U.S. as *Arabel's Raven*)
1977	*The Faithless Lollybird*
1979	*Arabel and Mortimer*
1979	*A Touch of Chill*
1982	*A Whisper in the Night*
1983	*Mortimer's Cross*
1984	*Up the Chimney Down*
1985	*Mortimer Says Nothing*
1985	*The Last Slice of Rainbow*
1986	*Past Eight O'Clock*

Plays

1972	*Winterthing*
1973	*The Mooncusser's Daughter*
1979	*Street*

Books for Adults (selected)

1964	*The Silence of Herondale*
1965	*The Fortune Hunters*
1967	*Hate Begins at Home* (in U.S. as *Dark Interval*)
1970	*The Embroidered Sunset*
1972	*Died on a Rainy Sunday*
1975	*Voices in an Empty House*
1977	*The Five Minute Marriage*
1978	*The Smile of a Stranger*
1980	*The Weeping Ash*
1982	*The Young Lady from Paris*
1982	*The Way to Write for Children*
1985	*Mansfield Revisited*
1987	*Deception* (in U.S. as *If I Were You*)
1989	*Blackground*

Lloyd Alexander

A t fifteen, in my last year of high school, I horrified my parents by announcing that I wanted to be an author. To save me from such a fate, they found me a respectable job as a bank messenger. After a couple of disastrous years, I quit and went briefly to a local college—equally disastrous. World War II had begun; so, hoping for excitement and adventure, I joined the army. In rapid and disheartening succession, I became an artilleryman, a cymbal player, a first-aid man, and a chapel organist. Appalled by my incompetence, as a last resort the army consigned me to military intelligence. Finishing training in Wales, I was posted to Alsace-Lorraine, the Rhineland, southern Germany, and, finally, to Paris. Discharged there, I attended the Sorbonne—a truant more often than not, for I was preoccupied with a beautiful Parisian girl, Janine. We married a few months later.

Though tempted to stay in Paris, I felt that if I wanted to write I should be where my roots were: Philadelphia, where I was born; Drexel Hill, where I grew up. Janine, her young daughter Madeleine, and I finally sailed home. I had two goals: to make a living and to write the world's greatest novel. As for making a living, I worked as a cartoonist, advertising writer, layout artist, and magazine editor. As for the world's greatest novel, indeed I wrote several, all thoroughly rejected. Seven years passed before I had a novel (not the world's greatest) published.

After some ten years of writing for adults, I wanted to write for young people. My instinct was right. Through the form of children's books, I could for the first time express my deepest feelings and concerns. It was the most creative and liberating experience of my life

5

While many of my books have been fantasies, I believe that fantasy is merely a way of reflecting attitudes about the real world. For example, the *Prydain Chronicles*—inspired by my stay in Wales and my long love of ancient mythology—try to show how we grow to become genuine human beings. As a corollary, the *Westmark Trilogy* deals with how we strive to keep our humanity in the midst of agonizingly difficult circumstances. Even in the *Vesper Holly Adventures*—written as humorous entertainments for myself as much as anyone—such themes lie not far below the lighthearted surface.

My books, to me, are very personal, one way or another drawing on my own experiences and observations. If they also speak to young adults, I'm delighted. Certainly no author could wish for better readers.

Bibliography

The Prydain Chronicles

1964   *The Book of Three*
1965   *The Black Cauldron*
1966   *The Castle of Llyr*
1967   *Taran Wanderer*
1968   *The High King*

The Westmark Trilogy

1981   *Westmark*
1982   *The Kestrel*
1984   *The Beggar Queen*

The Vesper Holly Adventures

1986   *The Illyrian Adventure*
1987   *The El Dorado Adventure*
1988   *The Drackenberg Adventure*
1989   *The Jedera Adventure*

Other Books for Young People

1958   *Border Hawk*
1960   *The Flagship Hope*
1963   *Time Cat*
1965   *Coll and His White Pig*

1967	*The Truthful Harp*
1970	*The Marvelous Misadventures of Sebastian*
1971	*The King's Fountain*
1972	*The Four Donkeys*
1973	*The Foundling*
1973	*The Cat Who Wished to Be a Man*
1975	*The Wizard in the Tree*
1977	*The Town Cats*
1978	*The First Two Lives of Lukas-Kasha*

Books for Adults

1955	*And Let the Credit Go*
1956	*My Five Tigers*
1958	*Janine is French*
1960	*My Love Affair with Music*
1962	*Park Avenue Vet*
1964	*Fifty Years in the Doghouse*

Judie Angell/Fran Arrick

H ere are some of the things in my category labelled "terrific" (not necessarily in order of importance): Living at the edge of a lake all year round. Anything by Stephen Sondheim. Capellini with tomato sauce. A good bargain. Word puzzles, all kinds except diagramless. My two kids. My two cats. My one husband. All the rest of my family, both sides. My house. Being able to pick my own work hours. Mel Torme. Cape Ann, Massachusetts. Anything written by John Irving or Pat Conroy. Sleeping late. Hot lunches. A check really in the mail. George Carlin. The *New York Magazine* Competition. A clean house. Laughing. Being with good friends. Being alone. When a plan really comes together. "L.A. Law." The kindness of strangers. Good health.

Here are my not-so-terrific things (not necessarily, etc.): Mail from insurance companies. "Vice President" Dan Quayle. The fact that teachers make so little and ballplayers make so much. And boxers. Especially boxers. A noise under the hood while you're driving. Morton Downey, Jr. Call-waiting. Waiting on line. Pop music written after 1955. The breakdown of society's values and home appliances. The fact that more money is spent by our government on military marching bands than on *all* of our country's cultural programs put together. Trying to park in New York City. Trying to park in Boston. Anything by Wagner. Root canal. That a lot of people really believe the kind of car one drives is important.

Bibliography

Judie Angell writes books for children under the name of Maggie Twohill, books for preteens and teenagers under the name of Judie Angell, and books for older teenagers under the name of Fran Arrick.

As Judie Angell

As Fran Arrick

As Maggie Twohill

Sandy Asher

I was born in Philadelphia and raised in a three-story row house by seven people: my grandparents, parents, aunt and uncle, and my brother, eight years older than I. My father was a doctor; his office took up half of the cramped first floor of our home. During office hours, in the afternoon and evening, we all had to be quiet.

I often spent that time alone in my room. I had my books, dolls, puppets, radio, a vast collection of fan magazines (we were all going to be movie stars in those days), and my imagination. I learned early that inner space was worth exploring. I cherish time alone to think, puzzle, ponder, daydream, and tell myself stories. Those solitary hours upstairs in my room were fine training for a writer.

On Sundays, my parents dropped me off at the Children's Reading Room entrance of the huge Free Library of Philadelphia. They drove off to visit their friends; I raced down the long ramp and through the tall glass doors to visit mine. Books. I adored their worn, dingy bindings all in a row and their musty smell. I believed wholeheartedly in the people within: Jo March, Peter Pan, Dorothy and the Scarecrow. They were so real and so dear to me, I thought that to write stories like the ones in which they lived had to be the most wonderful thing in the world to do.

It is. Summer, Jenny, Heather, Michael, and the other characters in my books are new friends as dear as the old.

It's great fun, but it isn't easy. If an actor doesn't show up for a performance, if a fire fighter quits in mid-fire, if a senator fails in his or her duties, people notice. One way or the other, they care. But if a writer doesn't write, or quits midway, or writes a book that's never published, the world goes on, blissfully unaware. If

Shakespeare had never written his plays, we would have been the poorer for it, but we wouldn't have known or cared.

A writer begins alone, proceeds alone, and can never be sure of what lies at the end of the journey. Many do it all with little or no encouragement. I was lucky. My teachers at Blaine Elementary School, Germantown High, and Indiana University recognized the path I had chosen, valued it, and cheered me on. I'm forever grateful to them.

Still, we all face each blank sheet of paper alone, with high hopes, yes, but also with fear: What if I have nothing worthwhile to say? Or what if I don't say it well enough? Or what if nobody cares? It takes considerable courage to type those words of commitment: Chapter One.

Where does that courage come from? From those childhood feelings of being connected to something wonderful. From teachers whose smiles of approval last a lifetime. From a passion for stories and respect for the written word. And from the understanding that, successful by others' standards or not, writers lead privileged lives, dedicated to work they love.

Bibliography

Books for Young Adults

1980	*Summer Begins* (now *Summer Smith Begins*)
1980	*Daughters of the Law*
1982	*Just Like Jenny*
1983	*Things Are Seldom What They Seem*
1984	*Missing Pieces*
1987	*Everything Is Not Enough*

Series

| 1989 | *Ballet One* |

Other Fiction

| 1985 | *Teddy Teabury's Fabulous Fact* |
| 1989 | *Teddy Teabury's Peanutty Problems* |

Nonfiction

| 1978 | *The Great American Peanut Book* |

Avi

I was born December 23, 1937, in New York City. That my twin sister is also a writer says much about the world I grew up in. For I come from a family of writers and a house full of books. Strange if we hadn't become writers.

Family legend has it that at five I rushed into a room shouting, "I can read!" Indeed, I came to read anything and everything. I loved reading then just as I do today. And I listened. How I loved to listen to family talk and radio adventures!

Watching, listening, reading: the natural education of a writer. One thing more: I thought of myself as an outsider. Took pride in it.

Was I then a *natural* writer? Hardly. Fridays—spelling test days—were dreaded days for me. Indeed, I flunked out of the first high school I went to, and almost the second. Truth is, I couldn't write, spell, punctuate. Wouldn't have made it without the help of a tutor. Years later I was to learn that I had dysgraphia, a writing dysfunction.

Not knowing that, insisting rather that I could write, by high school senior days I'd made up *my* stubborn mind: I was going to be a writer.

It was never easy. Lots of family discouragement. But a few key outside supporters. I was a playwright first but met with little success. I turned to the adult novel. Not much success there either. Only when my own kids came into my life did I start to write for young people. I was to find what I did best. Writing for kids has been at the center of my life ever since. Kids, if you will, gave me my life.

Whereas the place I am living has much to do with what I write (*The Fighting Ground, Something Upstairs*), only a few of my books (*S.O.R. Losers, Wolf Rider*) are based on things I've done. Instead, it's my feelings I feed on. Hence, *Bright Shadow,* a fantasy, is perhaps the most personal of my books. No wonder it took fourteen years!

What I always seek is a good, suspenseful story, rich in emotions, contradiction, irony—a story that grabs, makes you want to race to the end. At the same time I'm working hard to make the characters and ideas stay with the readers long after the last page.

I write slowly, quickly. Many, many rewrites. A word here. There. Shifting lines. Changing rhythms. Moving bit by bit, word by word, reaching toward an impossible balance of tone, tempo, tension. This very piece will no doubt see some thirty revisions.

Mind, I love to write. To write simply about things that are complex, to be able to evoke a sense of place, passion, caring. Hard? You bet. For me it always has been. I suspect it always will. *Hey, it gets harder.* Maybe I get more demanding.

But is there anything more fun than working—writing and rewriting—eight hours a day? I haven't found it.

Oh, yes, that name. My sister gave it to me.

Bibliography

Books for Young Adults

1977   *Captain Grey*
1979   *Night Journeys*
1980   *History of Helpless Harry*
1980   *Encounter at Easton*
1981   *A Place Called Ugly*
1982   *Sometimes I Think I Hear My Name*
1983   *Shadrach's Crossing*
1984   *The Fighting Ground*
1984   *Devil's Race*
1985   *Bright Shadow*
1986   *Wolf Rider*
1988   *Something Upstairs*
1989   *The Man Who Was Poe*
1990   *Seahawk*

Books for Younger Readers

1970   *Things That Sometimes Happen*

Jay Bennett

I sit at my typewriter, working on this autobiography, and I'm listening to Brahms' Violin Concerto and I ask myself, Why do I love music? Why do I love art? Why do I love literature? Why do I despise Sylvester Stallone and his Rambo creation?

Why have I always hated injustice and violence?

Why?

Memory flickers and I am back during the Depression riding a freight train and it is winter night and a winter rain is falling. I sit huddled in a corner of the boxcar, keeping to myself, and I watch two fellows getting worked up over nothing at all, really nothing, and soon they are on their feet swinging at each other and the train lurches and one of them is hit hard and he staggers and then the train lurches again and he is knocked out of the car, through the open door and down, goes toppling down a rock gully, to a sure death.

The rain keeps falling, and nobody says anything and then we start rolling over flat land, flat desert land, and soon all the fellows in the boxcar start jumping off the train and soon I am the last one left.

Then lightning flashes and a roll of harsh thunder and I slowly get up and go to the open door.

I jump and hit the wet dirt and tumble over and then get to my feet, the cold winter rain falling over me, going right through my clothes and into my very soul.

It's been there ever since.

I was born in New York City on December 24, 1912. My father, Pincus Shapiro, came over from Czarist Russia with thirteen cents in his pocket. My mother, Estelle Bennett, was born in New York City.

I have four brothers and one sister.
I am the only writer in the family.
Why this is so, I can't answer.
Why does one become a writer?
You tell me.
I'm ready to listen.

I do know that at the age of eighteen I decided to devote my life to writing. I then, for fourteen straight years, wrote steadily. Six novels, eight full-length stage plays, lots of poems, and many, many short stories.

And in all that long, dreary time, I never got one single word of encouragement. Not one little note from a publisher, a producer, an editor saying I had some talent and should keep on writing.

Then I met a writer who told me that a radio program, "Grand Central Station," was buying half-hour dramas. I sat down and wrote each day for twenty-seven days a drama. The twenty-seventh was accepted and I was launched.

I wrote for all the networks and then when television came in, I did almost a million words for that medium. Then television moved to the West Coast. I went out there, did not find it my cup of tea, as they say, and came back to New York. I wrote some adult suspense novels and then got into the young adult field and have been in it ever since.

Why write for young adults?

Well, all through my years I have been intensely interested in the young, their problems and their hopes. Their dreams and despairs. My wife, who is married to me for more than fifty years, and my two children, one who is an architect and the other a doctor of education, say that I am still a child who will never really grow up.

And that's why it's so easy for me to write books for that readership. But there's more to it than that.

I feel very strongly that it's up to the young to help turn things around. We can't go on much longer the way we are.

When I was young, you had to grow up arithmetically. You did that and you were able to make some sense out of life. But today with the world, a pretty sick and chaotic one at that, hovering on the edge of extinction, the young have to grow up geometrically. Their perceptions must be deeper and quicker. Their grasp of essential knowledge swift and sure. Their search for truth pure and inviolate. In a word they must grow up fast and mature fast . . .

Or they're lost.
That's why I write for them.
And will continue to write for them.

Bibliography

Books for Young Adults

1968   *Deathman, Do Not Follow Me*
1969   *The Deadly Gift*
1972   *The Killing Tree*
1972   *Masks: A Love Story*
1973   *The Long Black Coat*
1974   *Shadows Offstage*
1974   *The Dangling Witness*
1976   *Say Hello to the Hit Man*
1977   *The Birthday Murderer*
1979   *The Pigeon*
1981   *Slowly, Slowly, I Raise the Gun*
1983   *The Executioner*
1984   *To Be a Killer*
1985   *I Never Said I Loved You*
1986   *The Skeleton Man*
1987   *The Haunted One*
1988   *Dark Corridor*
1989   *Sing Me a Death Song*

Books for Adults

1959   *Catacombs*
1963   *Murder Money*
1965   *Death Is a Silent Room*

Plays

1949   *No Hiding Place*
1951   *Lions After Slumber*

T. Ernesto Bethancourt

I am actually the rightful heir to the throne of the mythical kingdom of Bulgravia, and was spirited from my cradle by Gypsies shortly after my birth, in 1932. In Brooklyn, New York, where there was once a brief but burgeoning market in slightly used babies, I was sold to my adoptive parents for $11.95. My mother still complains that the Gypsies got the best of the bargain.

Despite my royal heritage, I attended New York City public schools, in the guise of a Puerto Rican truckdriver's son. It was a great lesson in democracy: street gangs and local hooligans bullied and pummeled me with the same élan as they did any other kid. Just as I was acquiring my neighborhood sobriquet of "The Walking Hematoma," my family moved to the rural outskirts of Tampa, Florida, where I had to deal only with rattlesnakes and alligators. I have fond memories of Florida, and incorporated some of them into my first novel, *New York City Too Far From Tampa Blues*.

When my family moved back to Brooklyn, I adopted a different method of survival. I hid out in the public library. It was there I discovered my own Shangri-La, as well as James Hilton's. After graduating from high school, I enlisted in the U.S. Navy, somewhat at the insistence of my parents, who'd had more than enough of my princely attitude, and also at the urging of local juvenile authorities, who felt the service would "straighten me out." I didn't even know I was crooked. While I was in the navy, the Korean War broke out. In consequence of the GI Bill, I became the first member of my family to attend a college, then The City College of New York, where I majored in English and minored in psychology and history. I had vague ambitions for a career in law.

19

At CCNY, I discovered that all the blues taught to me by my Uncle Jack, and those I'd learned to sing and play on my guitar, were actually folk songs. I further learned that people would pay a lot of money to hear me perform. I dropped out of college at the beginning of my senior year and began a career as a performer/songwriter that was to last until I was forty-one years old.

When the McCarthy madness hit its height, I moved to Paris, where I lived for two years, returning only when John F. Kennedy was elected to the presidency. The folk music boom was full upon the nation and my career flourished. After the boom went bust, I stayed on, writing and performing social satire at chichi nightclubs across the country and in Canada. In 1970, when performing at The Ice House in Pasadena, California, I met and married a beautiful Japanese-American lady, Nancy Yasue Soyeshima. In 1974, in New York City, the first of our two daughters, Kimi, was born, followed the next year by Dorothea. The girls are named for their grandmothers.

When Kimi was born, I was forty-one years old. It entered my mind that by the time she would be an adolescent, and might wonder about her daddy's background, I could very well be dead. I began writing an autobiography in hopes that one day she'd read it. Through a series of extraordinary events, the autobiography became novelized, updated, and was published in 1975 as . . . *Tampa Blues*. The book was an immense success, and I began a new career in mid-life. Since then, twenty hardcover editions of my novels for young adults have been published, TV films have been based on them, and I have become a full-fledged author, albeit accidentally.

Considering the fact that my father died a functional illiterate, and that my mother had an eighth-grade education, I must attribute my success as a writer to the New York City Public School System and the New York Public Library. I thank them, every day, for the new and wonderful life they have given to me and my family.

Bibliography

Books for Young Adults

1975   *New York City Too Far From Tampa Blues*
1976   *The Dog Days of Arthur Cane*
1977   *The Mortal Instruments*
1978   *Dr. Doom: Superstar*

1979	*Tune in Yesterday*
1979	*Nightmare Town*
1979	*Instruments of Darkness*
1981	*Where the Deer and the Cantaloupe Play*
1983	*T.H.U.M.B.B.*
1984	*The Tomorrow Connection*
1984	*The Great Computer Dating Game*
1985	*The Me Inside of Me*
1989	*Googie*

Series

| 1980–84 | Doris Fein mysteries |

Judy Blume

O f all the characters I've created in my books, I am most like Sally, the ten-year-old heroine of *Starring Sally J. Freedman as Herself.* I grew up in Elizabeth, New Jersey, in a red brick house on a suburban street. My father, whom I adored, was a dentist. He was fun-loving, exciting, and passed his philosophy of life on to me: *Make every day count.* My mother, who had once been a legal secretary, stayed at home to take care of the house and my older brother, David, and me. She was shy and quiet, a worrier, who never talked to me about life.

I had a very active fantasy life as a child. In my fantasy life I could do or be anything I wanted. I loved making up stories inside my head. I never told anyone about them, though. I thought if I did I would be considered weird.

In high school I thought seriously about studying acting. My father encouraged me, as always, but my mother's wishes were far more practical and acceptable for the mid-fifties. By the time I left for college I had decided she was probably right. I would study education instead, find a husband, settle down, and have babies. I did exactly that. And without very many second thoughts.

I can't say exactly when or why I decided to write. It was just something that happened, perhaps out of desperation, for something was missing from my life—that creative intensity I needed in order to thrive. I loved my children but somewhere along the way I had lost myself.

Once I began to write, at age twenty-seven, I was determined to write the kinds of books that weren't there for me when I was growing up. Books about real life and real feelings. I think I wrote about young people because at the time it seemed to me that everything was possible at twelve, and at twenty-seven it was not.

I set my books in places that are real to me—the Northeast suburbs (where I was raised), New Mexico (where I lived for seven years), and New York City (where I live now). Many ideas come from my own life. In *Are You There God? It's Me, Margaret,* I wrote about my feelings and concerns when I was in sixth grade; in *Tiger Eyes,* my father's sudden death; in *Smart Women,* falling in love again at forty. But even though a basic idea may come from real life, the telling comes from the imagination. I never know what's going to happen when I begin to write a book. The pleasure for me is in finding out.

Writing changed my life. It allowed me to develop, to grow, to change. It brought me freedom. It helped me see that life is as full of possibilities today as it once seemed to be at age twelve.

Bibliography

Books for Young Adults

1970	*Are You There God? It's Me, Margaret*
1971	*Then Again Maybe I Won't*
1972	*It's Not the End of the World*
1972	*Otherwise Known as Sheila the Great*
1973	*Deenie*
1975	*Forever*
1981	*Tiger Eyes*
1981	*The Judy Blume Diary*
1987	*Just as Long as We're Together*

Books for Younger Readers

1969	*The One in the Middle Is the Green Kangaroo*
1970	*Iggie's House*
1971	*Freckle Juice*
1972	*Tales of a Fourth Grade Nothing*
1974	*Blubber*
1977	*Starring Sally J. Freedman as Herself*
1980	*Superfudge*
1984	*The Pain and the Great One*

Books for Adults

| 1978 | *Wifey* |

1983   *Smart Women*

Other Books

1986   *Letters to Judy: What Kids Wish They Could Tell You*
1988   *The Judy Blume Memory Book*

Larry Bograd

PHOTO: S. STEPHEN HICKS

I decided to become a writer at age nineteen, when I wrote my first novel. But I backed into writing for children and young adults by getting a job at a children's book company in 1977, when I finished graduate school and moved to New York City to learn how the publishing industry worked. The company, Harvey House, has since gone out of business, but while there I wrote a picture book, *Felix in the Attic*, for my friend, the illustrator Dirk Zimmer. It became each of our first published books.

Growing up in Denver, Colorado, I knew from an early age that I wanted to do something different and be my own boss. At first I considered being an astronaut, then an artist, then a politician, then an actor—and finally an author. (I always liked the idea of writing books, as opposed to articles or stories.) As a kid I didn't read much fiction, mostly history and biographies and science books, wishing to learn about the *real* world.

My father was born in eastern Europe, grew up in Newark, New Jersey, and met my mother in New York City, her hometown. They moved out west after my dad finished his medical training. As a family, we used to take summer-long car trips, exploring most of the United States. So I grew up exposed to many different people and places, open to new experiences and sensibilities.

When I was a teenager, two things happened which shaped my life and what I write about. The death of my father, when I was thirteen, made me understand how fragile life and family can be: a sense of loss, of how things should have been, can be found in much of my writing. And being a teenager in the late 1960s and early 1970s when Malcolm X, Robert Kennedy, and Martin Luther King, Jr., were gunned down, when American cities erupted in riots, and even a large popular opposition couldn't stop the war in Vietnam—these events gave me a moral anger (I like to think) about the hypocrisy of authority—again, a theme found in much of my work.

As with many writers, episodes and emotional memories anchor my novels. *The Kolokol Papers, Los Alamos Light,* and *Travelers* each deal with a teenager coping with the loss of a parent. Further, *The Kolokol Papers* drew on my own travels to the Soviet Union and my eastern European heritage; *Los Alamos Light* and *Travelers* reflect my love of the American West. *Bad Apple* was written after I had worked at a runaway shelter in Times Square, New York City. *The Better Angel* was based in part on my own senior year in high school.

Three of my young adult novels—*Bad Apple, The Better Angel,* and *Travelers*—have been attacked by censors and removed from library shelves. My work often deals with harsh political and emotional realities because I write the sort of books I wish I'd found as a teenager: no sugar coating, no mindless entertainment, but material that would make me think and see the world for the complicated place it often is. So my only rule for any serious writer is to tell the truth, the full truth—and how other people deal with it is their responsibility.

Bibliography

Books for Young Adults

1981	*The Kolokol Papers*
1982	*Bad Apple*
1983	*Los Alamos Light*
1985	*The Better Angel*
1986	*Travelers*

Books for Younger Readers

1986	*Poor Gertie*
1987	*Bernie Entertaining*
1989	*The Fourth-Grade Dinosaur Club*
1990	*Just Say No*

Picture Books

1979   *Felix in the Attic,* illus. by Dirk Zimmer
1980   *Egon,* illus. by Dirk Zimmer
1981   *Lost in the Store,* illus. by Victoria Chess

Robin F. Brancato

PHOTO: CAROL KITMAN

I have wanted to be a writer for as long as I can remember. I spent my growing-up years, from the ages of four to fifteen, in a suburb called Wyomissing, near Reading, Pennsylvania. Wyomissing was then and is now a wonderful place for children. Within walking distance from my house were a school I loved, a good library, a playground and swimming pool, woods and a creek to explore, and a main street with lots of shops. Although I was active and sociable as a child, I also liked to be alone—to read, and write, and listen to the radio. My first novel, *Don't Sit Under the Apple Tree*, is set in a fictional town that resembles Wyomissing.

When I was fifteen I was uprooted. My father was transferred by the company he worked for, and I suddenly found myself (along with my parents, brother, and sister) in Shamokin, Pennsylvania, a coal-mining town. I suffered. I missed my friends. I kept having fantasies about moving back "home." The pain of this separation later became part of my second novel, *Something Left to Lose*. Eventually I adjusted to Shamokin, just in time to move on to Camp Hill High School, also in Pennsylvania. I came to value, years later, the broadening effects of these moves, but at the time, I often felt sorry for myself and tried to bury that sorrow in writing and in reading books. Some of the titles that made the biggest impression on me then were *Grapes of Wrath*, by John Steinbeck, *Gone With the Wind*, by Margaret Mitchell, *Rebecca*, by Daphne duMaurier, and *The Thirteen Clocks*, by James Thurber.

In college, at the University of Pennsylvania, I majored in creative writing. Not only did I write a lot, as a result, but I also learned to accept criticism. And then, after graduation from Penn, I took a not-so-pleasant waitressing job for the summer, in order to save up enough money to make a three-month trip to Europe. When I returned, I went to New York City to join two college friends in sharing an apartment. My first full-time job was as a copy editor of technical textbooks.

I didn't stay long in this position. It immediately struck me that it's much more interesting to go through books looking for ideas rather than for misspelled words. So, the obvious solution was to become an English teacher. And then, about 1973, I began the juggling act I still practice—teaching part of the time and writing whenever I can. As it has turned out, my teaching experiences and my students have been the major influences on my writing, especially in such novels as *Winning, Come Alive at 505,* and *Uneasy Money.* In both my teaching and my writing I try to do the same thing: raise questions I may not know the answers to, questions that will make people think.

At present I live with my husband in Teaneck, New Jersey, where I teach in the mornings and write in the afternoons. Another influence on my work has been my two sons, both now grown up. One is a screenwriter, the other an investigator.

Bibliography

1975	*Don't Sit Under the Apple Tree*
1976	*Something Left to Lose*
1977	*Winning*
1978	*Blinded by the Light*
1980	*Come Alive at 505*
1982	*Sweet Bells Jangled Out of Tune*
1984	*Facing Up*
1986	*Uneasy Money*

Robbie Branscum

I was raised in the Arkansan hills by grandparents, as children were a hundred years ago. I went to school in a small one-room schoolhouse until the seventh grade, and fell in love with books. I am greedy for them. When I was thirteen my mother moved me to Colorado, next door to a one-room library, and that's where I finished my schooling and can never praise libraries enough.

Bibliography

1971   Me and Jim Luke
1975   Johnny May
1975   The Three Wars of Billy Joe Treat
1976   Toby, Granny and George
1977   The Saving of P.S.
1978   Toby Alone
1978   Toby and Johnny Joe
1978   Three Buckets of Daylight
1978   The Ugliest Boy
1978   For Love of Jody
1978   To the Tune of a Hickory Stick
1982   The Murder of Hound Dog Bates
1983   Spud Tackett and the Angel of Doom
1983   Cheater and Flitter Dick
1984   The Adventures of Johnny May
1986   The Girl
1987   Johnny May Grows Up
1989   Cameo Rose

Sue Ellen Bridgers

PHOTO: BEN BRIDGERS

I grew up in a small eastern North Carolina town in the middle of tobacco country. Most of the people in Winterville were involved in farming and our lives were quite rural although my family lived in town, close to church and school. I grew up with two siblings, a sister Sandra two years older, and a brother Abbott almost six years younger. We lived in a house beside our grandmother. On the other side and behind us lived uncles. Our paternal grandmother lived a few blocks away. So we were surrounded by family.

My grandmother Abbott, who lived next door, was a wonderful storyteller. She had had a great deal of sadness in her life and she relived those times frequently. She had also had fun and she told those stories as well. Growing up at Renston, which was her general theme, has become as important in my writing world as my own childhood experiences.

Because I lived in an extended family of farmers, our connection to the land and to the history of a place was always important. Farm children paid attention to the weather, and the changing seasons had special importance to us. The natural world found a place in my writing quite early, and I still try to be responsive to visual experience. Today, instead of just thinking how beautiful a tree is, I ask myself to mentally describe it.

I graduated from the local high school and went to college in a neighboring town, only seven miles away. After three years in college, where I studied English and worked for the literary magazine, I married an instructor in the English department. I left school at the end of my junior year when Ben decided to join the air force. Our two daughters were born while we were in the service. Our son was born during Ben's first year in law school at the University of

North Carolina. I didn't finish college until 1976 after we had moved to Sylva, North Carolina, and our youngest had started school. That same year, my first book, *Home Before Dark*, was published. *Home Before Dark* is the story of a migrant girl coming to live in a community much like the one in which I grew up. To write it, I had to draw on my own childhood experiences and my family's attachment to the land.

Since *Home Before Dark*, I have written two other books set in eastern North Carolina. Then in 1981, I began a book called *Sara Will*, which takes place in a fictional town called Tyler Mills. In that book I envisioned Tyler Mills in the lower mountains of North Carolina. Since then I have written another book with Tyler Mills as the setting. This time Tyler Mills is truly in the mountains where I have lived since 1971. It's one of the privileges of fiction to be able to move towns around!

The most exciting part of my writing life is discovering the characters themselves, which is much like getting to know a real person. I spend a long time, usually at least a year, thinking about the characters who will people a book. After that, when I feel I can trust the main characters to tell their stories, I begin the writing, which usually goes rather quickly. This process—a year of thinking about the characters, a year of writing the story, a year in the publication process—has been productive for me, and I hope to continue this method of work.

Bibliography

1976   *Home Before Dark*
1979   *All Together Now*
1981   *Notes for Another Life*
1985   *Sara Will*
1987   *Permanent Connections*

Bruce Brooks

I started becoming a writer when I started reading. I don't mean only that I developed an interest in books—I mean that I started making things up in words, alternative stories that went along with the ones I was reading. I cannot recall a time—even back when I was doing the Look-Jane-Look bit in the first grade—in which I did not play with the text this way. Upon opening my first book in Miss Kirby's class at Highland View Elementary School I thought, *Somebody wrote this. I bet I could do it, too.* The taking-in of one tale from the page and the making-up of another in my head were inseparable parts of the same experience for me, and it was all quite natural.

It was natural not because I was a prodigy; it was natural because I was a kid. It's simply a universal confidence and creativity kids have. If they like something, they want to make their own versions. My five-year-old son records tapes of himself singing Talking Heads songs while hammering a Fisher-Price xylophone, and draws his own ice hockey trading cards with Piglet as a goalie and Pooh as a left wing; so it was with me and books. I murmured my own Dick and Spot stories, and my own Tarzan stories, and my own Crusader Rabbit stories as I read. The books did not seem to mind. The words on the page stood more for enthusiastic suggestions of possibilities than immutable facts. I felt invited to collaborate, to ring my own changes.

Things got harder as my reading progressed. A six-year-old does a better job of ringing changes on "SEE SPOT JUMP!" than a twelve-year-old does on five hundred pages of *Great Expectations.* So I started writing my own stuff from scratch. This was much easier than dreaming up new twists for Huck or Pip or Batman.

No teacher ever saw my writing, but if one had read something such as *The Golf Course At Night* (a title I recall), he or she would have looked ahead to my future and said, "This boy, someday, is going to make an absolutely first-rate *accountant*." Or third-rate auto mechanic, or something—anything but a writer, because the stories were so awful no one would have given me a hope. But the important thing, I suppose, was that I had the initiative to write them. I was not impatient. I knew they were bound to be bad for a while. I just kept practicing. And after only twenty more years of practice (who's counting?), I was ready to write a novel, which turned out to be *The Moves Make the Man*.

The reader-writer business is still at the heart of my work. The converse of my first reading experiences is now true: then I read as a writer, now I write as a reader. I sit at my typewriter making up the story with all of my technical manipulation of language and ideas, and I simultaneously devour the story as a reader, and demand more. The two actions are still inseparable—two senses, as it were, of one awareness. I seem to need both. The suspense and foresight of my reading really keep my writing going: I am peering over my own shoulder going *Yeah? And then? Wow! And what happens next? Ooh—think you can pull that idea off, hotshot?*

Having my first three books marketed for kids has been a real blessing. But I don't write with kids in mind as readers. I don't have any classification of readers in mind when I write, or any faceless Ideal Reader archetype—I am reader enough for the moment. I'm happy my books are read by kids, though, because reading *matters* so much to kids, and thus they invest more in it, and thus I get what every writer really wants: hardworking readers who are ready to be inspired.

I don't feel I write books *about* kids, exactly; I feel I write books about families and friends—ultimately (this sounds corny) about love and the way it works between people. Are there five writers in the history of the world who cannot say the same thing?

Bibliography

Books for Young Adults

1984   *The Moves Make the Man*
1986   *Midnight Hour Encores*
1989   *No Kidding*

Nonfiction

1989   *On the Wing*

Eve Bunting

PHOTO: CHRISTINE BUNTING

I was born and grew up in Maghera, a little town in County Derry, Ireland.

Ireland is known for its lush, green beauty, and believe me, the reason for that lush beauty is because there is lots of rain. It's strange, though. When I think back to my childhood, all I can remember are sunny days and my mother saying to me, "Take your head out of that book, lovey, and go outside before it starts pouring again." I was an only child, a reader, and a listener.

My father was a tough, down-to-earth Irishman with a secret passion—for poetry. I was his audience. He loved the tenderness of W. B. Yeats. "I will arise and go now, and go to Innisfree," he'd say dreamily as we sat by the turf fire. "Listen to the words, darlin'. Listen to the sounds of them."

I listened. And I think it was from my father that I got my respect for the sounds words make, my delight in their rhythms.

As many Irish children do, I went early to boarding school in the big city of Belfast, leaving home and parents at the age of seven. I cried night after night, wanting my mother above all, scared and lonely and homesick. But one toughens in boarding school. Boarding schools pride themselves in the toughening process. It was World War II and Belfast was being bombed. Rationing was a good excuse for poor quality food . . . I still can't eat sausages! A shortage of fuel was a good reason for cold baths and inadequate heating. We got tougher by the day.

But there were good friends, too: girls who became sisters to me and are sisters still. Some day I will write a book about those days and about them.

I met my husband-to-be at Queen's University, in an English literature class. Many factors, economic and philosophical, combined

36

to convince us to emigrate to the United States with our three small children in 1958. Anyone who thinks that kind of decision is easy has never done it. Pulling up from the past is agonizing. But leaving Ireland seems to be one of the things the Irish do best.

It was many years later, when my youngest child was in junior high, that I began writing. My first book, *The Two Giants*, was published in 1972. It tells of the Irish giant Finn McCool and the Scottish giant Culcullan and the laying of the Giant's Causeway, a wonder of the world located just eighteen miles from my home in Maghera.

Two of my novels have Irish settings also: *The Haunting of Kildoran Abbey* and *Ghost of Summer*, and I often use Maghera for picture book backgrounds. *Clancy's Coat* has as a main character a tailor who could have been the one who lived on the Glen Road and who promised everything for tomorrow and hid in the cow shed when he saw you coming!

But many of my books reflect my good, new life, too, with contemporary California themes and atmosphere: *If I Asked You, Would You Stay?* and *A Sudden Silence*, which deals with a crisis in the life of a teenage surfer. Maghera was not much noted for its surfing, in my day or now.

I see little rain in California. But never mind. There are still books waiting to be read and written under the sunshine skies. And always there is the memory of Innisfree.

Bibliography

Books for Young Adults

1976   One More Flight
1977   Ghost of Summer
1978   The Haunting of Kildoran Abbey
1979   The Cloverdale Switch
1982   The Ghosts of Departure Point
1984   If I Asked You, Would You Stay?
1984   Surrogate Sister
1985   The Haunting of Safekeep
1985   Face at the Edge of the World
1987   Will You Be My POSSLQ?
1988   A Sudden Silence

Other Books

Alice Childress

I was born in Charleston, South Carolina, and was raised and educated among the people of Harlem, New York, the genteel poor. They are the people I tend to write about—the "intellectual poor" who live and face trouble with humor and grace, and struggle forward in spite of deep anger and pain. Before I started writing novels, I worked in the theater, first as an actress for eleven years with the American Negro Theatre, both on and off Broadway, and then as a director and playwright. In 1966 I received a Harvard appointment as playwright/scholar to the Radcliffe Institute for Independent Study and was graduated from Radcliffe/Harvard in 1968. In 1984 I received the Radcliffe Alumnae Medal for distinguished achievement.

I wrote my first novel for young adults after Ferdinand Monjo, editor–vice president of Coward McCann and children's book author, suggested that I write a book about drugs because it was needed. So I wrote *A Hero Ain't Nothin' But a Sandwich*. My books for young adults deal with characters who feel rejected and have to painfully learn how to deal with other people, because I believe all human beings can be magnificent once they realize their full importance.

When I'm writing, characters seem to come alive; they move my pen to action, pushing, pulling, shoving, and intruding. I visualize each scene as if it were part of a living play. At times I get up and walk around the room, acting out the parts, because my theater writing influences my novel writing. I am pleased when readers say that my novels feel like plays, because it means they are very visual.

In addition to writing, I have been a member and council member of the Dramatists Guild, Writers of America East, the Authors League, PEN Club, and the Harlem Writers Guild.

Bibliography

Books for Young Adults

1973   *A Hero Ain't Nothin' But a Sandwich*
1981   *Rainbow Jordan*
1989   *Those Other People*

Books for Younger Readers

1975   *When Rattlesnake Sounds*
1976   *Let's Hear It for the Queen*

Books for Adults

1956   *Like One of the Family: Conversations from a Domestic's Life*
1979   *A Short Walk*
1987   *Many Closets*

Stage Plays

1949   *Florence*
1950   *Gold through the Trees*
1955   *Trouble in Mind*
1969   *String*
1969   *Young Martin Luther King* (music by Nathan Woodard)
1970   *Mojo: A Black Love Story*
1972   *Wedding Band*
1977   *Sea Island Song* (music by Nathan Woodard)
1986   *Moms: A Praise Play for a Black Comedienne*

Screenplays

1978   *A Hero Ain't Nothin' But a Sandwich*

Television Plays

1969   *Wine in the Wilderness*
1973   *Wedding Band*
1979   *String*

Vera A. Cleaver

PHOTO: GEORGE FLOWERS

I have never taken a writing course. I don't believe that anyone can teach another how to write. I believe that writing must be self-taught. I am a full-time, self-taught fiction writer. I don't have a degree in anything. Bill Cleaver was fond of saying that he and I graduated from the libraries of the United States of America.

Since Bill's death I live alone in a free-standing home in a small central Florida town. I see almost no one and go almost nowhere. My work, the daily hours I spend talking, talking, talking only to my typewriter, means isolation, and I am comfortable with this. I find a curious kind of strength in it. It reminds me that I can be, that I am, self-sufficient.

I learned about self-sufficiency as a child on a prairie farm in South Dakota. We had lived in Nebraska and Wyoming, but not as farmers. My father had been a station agent and then a traveling auditor for railroads in those states, so the farm in South Dakota was an education for all of us.

My memories of our life on the farm are clear and good. There was the big yellow house and the dirt road that ran past it, barns, a plum orchard, a windmill, grainfields, fruit and vegetable gardens.

41

Our nearest neighbors, miles distant, were German-Russians, good people anybody would want to know. At harvest time they came to help us. In turn, we went to help them, but beyond that we seldom saw them. We were severely isolated. A trip to town was an event.

We had to learn farming and how to live on a farm. It was there that my affection for plant life began, I think. I was given a handful of popcorn seed and a bucket of potato eyes and was shown how to plant them. That there exists a serious resemblance and serious relationship between human and plant life became a belief then. Bill shared this belief. It seeped into all of the writing we coauthored. It seeps into all the writing I now produce alone. I can't get away from it.

I was taught how to read and write before I started my formal schooling. My textbooks were those that had been used by my parents. My maternal grandfather, a newspaper publisher, and my paternal grandfather, a medical doctor, brought or sent others. We created our own social life. On winter nights my oldest sister told ghost stories and then, before bedtime, we gathered around the parlor piano to sing the songs my father played for us.

I was maybe seven years old when I started writing little stories and plays. I was the fifth of nine rambunctious children, so my creative writing efforts went largely unnoticed. That they were not celebrated or endlessly discussed was a matter of indifference to me. In that strange way that young children know things they haven't yet been taught, I knew that I was going to be a writer. This was not unique. Most of us who earn our livings at writing do know at a very early age, I think, that we will spend all of our lives at writing. We also know, or we find out, that we must apprentice for the job.

When I met and married Bill I was writing some pretty lofty stuff. Several editors had offered encouragement along with their rejections, but their suggestions for revision were vague. Bill was specific. He asked me how many rich people I had known and how was it I knew about jewel thieving? I had to confess that I had never known any rich people and knew nothing of any kind of thieving.

Bill took charge. In our first home, an attic apartment in Seattle, he and I began to write of things we knew. We wrote family stories, first for the pulp magazines and then for the slicks. We were Sunday writers. Both of us had jobs because writers too must eat and wear clothes and live in houses.

We stayed with the pulp magazines too long. Writing for them teaches discipline, as does all writing, but substantially the pulp magazine stories are formula. Slick magazines offer a better fare to their readers and better treatment to their writers.

Bibliography

Books for Young Adults by Vera and Bill Cleaver

1967	*Ellen Grae*
1968	*Lady Ellen Grae*
1969	*Where the Lilies Bloom*
1970	*Grover*
1970	*The Mimosa Tree*
1971	*I Would Rather Be a Turnip*
1971	*The Mock Revolt*
1972	*Delpha Green & Co.*
1973	*The Whys & Wherefores of Littabelle Lee*
1973	*Me Too*
1975	*Dust of the Earth*
1977	*Trial Valley*
1978	*Queen of Hearts*
1979	*A Little Destiny*
1981	*The Kissimmee Kid*
1983	*Hazel Rye*

Books for Young Adults by Vera Cleaver

1984	*Sugar Blue*
1985	*Sweetly Sings the Donkey*
1987	*Moon Lake Angel*
1988	*Belle Pruitt*

Christopher Collier

From the time I was eight years old I grew up in a small Connecticut town full of cows and orchards. I got to live the last glimmer of rural life in what was soon to become modern suburbia. I got to go skinny-dipping in the Norwalk River, shoot crows with a .22 rifle, and live out of earshot of automobiles and other people's radios.

When I was about fourteen years old I read Irving Stone's *They Also Ran* (I still have the very same copy), a collection of short biographies of presidential candidates who lost. That is the first history I recall reading for fun, but ever since then I have made the study of history my principal concern. Having grown up during the Great Depression in what used to be called "straitened circumstances," I was attracted to the idea of doing something that brought a steady paycheck. That meant teaching history, an objective I decided upon as a sophomore in high school.

It was when I was teaching eighth-grade American history that I was inspired to write historical novels. Surely there must be a better—more interesting and memorable—way to teach such exciting stuff as history is made of than through the dull, dull textbooks we used. My brother had already written some novels for teenagers, and after about fifteen years of my hounding him, he finally agreed to help me out. The result was *My Brother Sam Is Dead*.

Oh, yes! I was born in New York City in 1930 and lived for a while on Long Island. I loved camping and woodcraft and became an Eagle Scout. In high school I played trumpet in the band and orchestra, wrote for the newspaper, and acted in every play that came along. I also was president of the student council. I went to Clark University in Worcester, Massachusetts, and spent a couple of years in the army, mostly playing in a band. I have a Ph.D. from

Columbia University and have taught school since 1955—junior and senior high, but mostly college.

I have written a number of very dull books for scholarly types to read, but those intended for youngsters I have done with my brother.

Bibliography

1974   *My Brother Sam Is Dead*
1976   *The Bloody Country*
1978   *The Winter Hero*
1981   *Jump Ship to Freedom*
1983   *War Comes to Willy Freeman*
1984   *Who Is Carrie?*

James Lincoln Collier

I was born in New York City in 1928, and raised in the city's suburbs. I come from a family of writers. My father was an editor and author of about a half-dozen books, mostly for children. An uncle and an aunt were also editors and writers. A cousin was a sportswriter; a brother-in-law, a writer of short fiction; and of course my brother Christopher is my collaborator on a number of books for young readers and our adult study of the Constitutional Convention, *Decision in Philadelphia.*

In a sense, then, I went into the family business, with romantic illusions about the writer's life. I knew it would not be easy, but it never really occurred to me to do anything else. I went to Hamilton College, did a stint in the army, and then moved into the requisite cold-water flat in Greenwich Village to begin writing. For six years I supported myself and a young family as a magazine editor, but by 1958, when I was not quite thirty, I quit my job and began freelancing. I have not drawn an honest paycheck since.

It has never been easy, especially as I had children to raise and educate, but the economic goad was critically important in teaching me that what I wrote had first of all to be interesting to real people. Illusions that I am an artist must be ignored. I have always insisted that I am not that distinguished creature, an "author," but a writer practicing a profession—a difficult and demanding one, but a profession nonetheless. My best-liked books have always been those written not out of a fiery vision but as a professional, using sleights of hand that took me years to discover and develop.

This does not mean that I do not write from my own emotions. Of course I do, as any writer must. Part of the trick, in my view, is the successful management of one's own feelings. As it happens, I am also a working jazz musician, and I find that improvising jazz and writing fiction are very much the same. Both require me to *perform*, using my imagination, my feelings, and a sound grasp of the techniques of the craft.

I also, as a professional, pride myself on being able to write in any medium. I have written magazine pieces, books, screenplays, novels, humor, reportage, personality profiles, and scholarly works in a variety of disciplines, including music, the social sciences, history, and much else.

I have many interests. I play jazz regularly, like sports, read a great deal, cook, travel a lot, and enjoy working around my country house. But writing is always first. It is the thing on which everything else depends. It is at the center of my life, and I cannot imagine not doing it.

Bibliography

Books for Young Adults with Christopher Collier

1974	*My Brother Sam Is Dead*
1976	*The Bloody Country*
1978	*The Winter Hero*
1981	*Jump Ship to Freedom*
1983	*War Comes to Willy Freeman*
1984	*Who Is Carrie?*

Books for Children and Young Adults

1967	*The Teddy Bear Habit*
1970	*Rock Star*
1971	*Why Does Everybody Think I'm Nutty?*
1972	*It's Murder at St. Basket's*
1976	*Give Dad My Best*
1983	*Planet of the Past*
1986	*When the Stars Begin to Fall*
1987	*Outside, Looking In*
1988	*The Winchesters*

Books for Adults

1960	*Fires of Youth*
1962	*Somebody Up There Hates Me*
1964	*The Hypocritical American*

Hila Colman

B eing a grandmother of seven, I am highly amused when I am addressed as "a juvenile writer." I am far from being a juvenile, although I spend a great many of my waking hours (possibly even in my dreams) thinking and writing about young people.

Why am I fascinated by teenagers? The answer is not simple. For one, I am lucky in that I look back on my own teenage years not with nostalgia, but with pleasure. They were good years for me, years that, compared to today's pitfalls, I suppose could be called wholesome, a rather loathesome word to teenagers. Drugs were not on the scene, and while there was some drinking, nice girls were not wimps if they did not go to bed with boys. We had dances, parties, picnics on the beach; we dated, some made out more than others; we had very good times with little risk. This all happened out on Long Island, which in those days was considered country, and we played tennis, went horseback riding, and went everywhere freely on our bikes.

But perhaps more important than my own memories is that for me the adolescent years are a time of crisis: what to choose, which way to go, evolving a new look at that strange adult world, seeing parents with a fresh eye, not just as Mom and Dad, but as persons with lives and dimensions of their own.

As anyone reading my books knows, I am intrigued by family relationships. And it is during those teenage years that to my eye those relationships can change dramatically. It is that drama that I like to write about: the crosscurrents are endless, the plots are endless. One can hardly pick up a magazine or newspaper without reading about a family in crisis that involves teenagers. And I don't mean necessarily drugs and crime; I mean divorces, adoption, custody fights, runaways, achievements, sibling problems, accidents, ill-

49

ness. . . . The drama is there for the taking, and I can bring my own perceptions, my own characters, and my own solutions to these open-ended situations. It is great fun to arrange these lives, the people I create, to my own (and I hope the reader's) satisfaction. Not that they all get happy endings; oh no, that would be too simple-minded, and my audience is far from naive.

As for the pertinent facts of my life: I live in rural Connecticut and recently have bought a simple house on a canal on the west coast of Florida that we use for about three winter months. I like to write some every day, in the morning. I do a great deal of walking, in the woods at home, on the beach in Florida. With my sons and their families and seven grandchildren, I have a rich family life and a close group of friends. I like to cook, I love movies, do a lot of reading, and hope that the ideas don't run dry. One guard against that is my own interest in politics and in what goes on in the world locally, nationally, and internationally. I have a list of organizations I support, environmental and peace groups; in my hometown I am chair of the Zoning Board of Appeals and a member of the Democratic Town Committee. I am also a member of the Authors Guild and of PEN and Amnesty International.

Bibliography

Books for Children and Young Adults (selected)

1957	*The Big Step*
1958	*A Crown for Gina*
1961	*The Girl from Puerto Rico*
1962	*Watch That Watch*
1963	*Peter's Brownstone House*
1969	*Claudia, Where Are You?*
1973	*Chicano Girl*
1973	*Diary of a Frantic Kid Sister*
1975	*Ethan's Favorite Teacher*
1976	*Nobody Has to Be a Kid Forever*
1977	*Sometimes I Don't Love My Mother*
1977	*The Case of the Stolen Bagels*
1978	*Tell Me No Lies*
1978	*Rachael's Legacy*
1979	*Ellie's Inheritance*
1980	*What's the Matter with the Dobsons?*

Ellen Conford

As a child, I loved to read. I began to write poems in elementary school, but did not take writing seriously until I began to have my work published in my high school paper and magazine.

My mother says she knew I was going to be a writer when I was in the third grade. For my part, I wanted to be an actress (at least until sixth grade).

My writing met with no success until 1968, when I began to receive acceptances, along with the usual rejections, of my short stories.

My first children's book was published in 1971. It's called *Impossible Possum*. As my own son grew, so did my books. I found that I enjoyed writing for young adults more than I'd enjoyed any other writing for kids. My early teen years were the most intense years of my life. I remember things so vividly, probably because the feelings in adolescence are so strong—the lows *so-o-o* low, and the highs stratospheric.

It's hard to describe how an idea for a book comes to me. Some books "just happen," and I never know how I thought them up. Some books were inspired by hearing an interesting name and then imagining what a character with that name would be like. I actually dreamed two of my books: *Lenny Kandell, Smart Aleck* and *To All My Fans, with Love from Sylvie*. The dreams were so real and so complete that when I woke up I felt they were stories I had to write. Only one of my books, *Hail, Hail Camp Timberwood*, is entirely based on my own experiences. The rest are mostly made up, although some of the things I write about did happen to me.

Growing up is hard—and a complicated process. Even though I am now (supposed to be) an adult, I often find that teenagers and adolescence are more interesting than grown-ups and maturity.

I live on Long Island with my husband, David, and a cat named Children's Room. My hobbies include reading, playing Scrabble, doing crossword puzzles, collecting old cookbooks, watching movies, and *eating*!

Bibliography

Books for Young Adults

1975   *Dear Lovey Heart, I Am Desperate*
1977   *The Alfred G. Graebner Memorial High School Handbook of Rules and Regulations*
1978   *Hail, Hail Camp Timberwood*
1979   *We Interrupt This Semester for an Important Bulletin*
1982   *Seven Days to a Brand New Me*
1982   *To All My Friends with Love from Sylvie*
1983   *If This Is Love, I'll Take Spaghetti*
1984   *You Never Can Tell*
1985   *Why Me?*
1985   *Strictly for Laughs*
1986   *A Royal Pain*
1987   *The Things I Did for Love*
1989   *Genie with the Light Blue Hair*

Series

1988–89 *Jenny Archer*

Books for Children

1971   *Impossible Possum*
1972   *Why Can't I Be William?*
1973   *Dreams of Victory*
1973   *Felicia the Critic*
1974   *Just the Thing for Geraldine*
1974   *Me and the Terrible Two*
1975   *The Luck of Pokey Bloom*
1977   *And This Is Laura*
1978   *Eugene the Brave*
1979   *Anything for a Friend*
1980   *The Revenge of the Incredible Dr. Rancid and His Youthful Assistant, Jeffrey*
1983   *Lenny Kandell, Smart Aleck*

Susan Cooper

PHOTO: BIRGIT BLYTH

I sound very English, they tell me, even though I've lived in the United States for more than twenty-five years. Well, I *am* very English: born and raised in the green Thames Valley, which was rather noisy at first because the bombs of World War II were falling. Strictly speaking, by blood I'm one-quarter Welsh; in the British Isles we are all mongrels.

Like most born scribblers, I edited the school magazine and the university newspaper; after that I spent seven rapturous years as a reporter and feature-writer for the London *Sunday Times.* In my spare time I wrote two novels, one of them a children's book called *Over Sea, Under Stone.* Then, to my editor's horror, I married an American widower with three teenage children, and went to live in the United States.

Ten homesick years later, after producing about four hundred weekly columns for a British newspaper, several books, and two babies, I suddenly discovered that *Over Sea* was meant to be the first in a sequence of five books, under the overall title of *The Dark Is Rising.* So I wrote the other four. They took me six-and-a-half years, and they dealt with the basic substance of myth, which has always haunted me: the complicated, ageless conflict between good and evil, the Light and the Dark. When children ask, as they constantly ask all authors, "Where do you get your ideas?", I think of the day when I discovered *The Dark Is Rising,* and I say, with aching honesty, "I don't know. I wish I did." Fantasy, like poetry, comes out of a part of your imagination that you can neither predict nor properly control.

After that sequence I wrote one other fantasy novel that the publishers classified as "young adult." It was called *Seaward,* and I'm fond of it. But for the most part, the fantasy-making side of my head decided it wanted to go into the theatre—which is itself a kind of fantasy. I wrote songs and small plays for a company called Revels, founded by John Langstaff, which has Christmas productions in six American cities, and I collaborated with the Canadian actor Hume Cronyn on *Foxfire*, a play which eventually ran for seven months on Broadway. After that I began, almost by accident, to write scripts for television films. The best so far are the television version of *Foxfire*, and a film called *The Dollmaker* for Jane Fonda, based on a wonderful book by Harriette Arnow.

I shall go on writing books, most of which will turn out to be fantasies for "young adults," and I shall go on writing plays and films for "adults" as well. I'm really one of those authors who belong back in an age before labels, when all storytellers produced folktales—for folk, which meant everyone. I love being able to try to make a magic: to make you laugh, or cry, or experience what Aristotle called a catharsis—which means, in effect, feeling better even though a story has slugged you on the back of the head.

And I guess every writer in this book would say the same. We are a fortunate bunch. We were given something, and in one way or another we spend our lives trying to give it to everyone else.

Bibliography

Books for Young Adults

1965	*Over Sea, Under Stone*
1970	*Dawn of Fear*
1973	*The Dark Is Rising*
1974	*Greenwitch*
1975	*The Grey King*
1977	*Silver on the Tree*
1983	*Seaward*

Books for Younger Readers

1979	*Jethro and the Jumbie*, illus. by Ashley Bryan
1983	*The Silver Cow*, illus. by Warwick Hutton
1986	*The Selkie Girl*, illus. by Warwick Hutton

Plays

| 1983 | *Foxfire* (with Hume Cronyn) |

Other Books

1963   *Age of Austerity 1945–51* (contributor)
1964   *Mandrake*
1965   *Behind the Golden Curtain: A View of the USA*
1968   *Essays of the Five Decades* [J. B. Priestley] (editor)
1970   *J. B. Priestley: Portrait of an Author*

Robert Cormier

PHOTO: FINKLE PHOTOGRAPHER

For thirty years of my life, I went around disguised as a newspaperman. I began as a street reporter, covering fires and accidents. Then, I recorded the daily politics of a lively New England city. Later, I wrote headlines, editorials, and human interest columns. The most unforgettable moment of my newspaper career was writing the headline—eight columns of 96-point type—announcing the death of President John F. Kennedy in Dallas. For a brief moment, I felt that I was a part of my country's history.

In my heart, however, I was never really a journalist but a novelist and a short story writer. After turning out my daily quota of paragraphs at the newspaper, I came home—and came alive. During the evenings and often late into the night, I did my *real* writing—stories, first, and later, novels. Nights and weekends my old Royal typewriter clattered and clanged as the words sang and danced on the page, although they sometimes stumbled or stalled. Newspaper writing confined me to the straitjacket of facts. In the cluttered little room in which I write even these words, my writing was like winged flight, as I created a world of my own and a town called Monument. Sitting at my typewriter, I have lived many lives—I have been Jerry Renault refusing to sell those chocolates and Kate Forrester trying to start that hostaged bus and Adam Farmer pedaling his bicycle toward an unknown destination. I have both laughed and wept while sitting here.

It astonishes some people when they learn that I still live in my hometown of Leominster, Massachusetts, three miles away from the house in which I was born. I attended local schools, worked after school in local stores, selling shoes and jerking sodas. I punched a time clock in Leominster factories—where combs and brushes were produced. Even then I was in disguise, going home at night to write stories with pencil and paper on the kitchen table.

Since 1978, I have been free of disguises, have been a full-time, every day novelist.

When I speak to students about writing, I hold myself up as an example of that ancient axiom—write about what you know. I also tell them that you don't have to be a genius or travel the seven seas to be a writer. Even though my novels have dealt with such topics as terrorism, government corruption, and medical experimentation, I could have written them without stepping outside of my hometown. I have traveled widely, have gone halfway around the world, but my travels have not provided the material for my novels. Here in Leominster, watching and listening, pondering the comings and goings of my hometown, I have seen a thousand novels unfold. I have managed, at this point, to write nine of them. Which leaves me 991 to go.

Bibliography

Books for Young Adults

1974	*The Chocolate War*
1977	*I Am the Cheese*
1979	*After the First Death*
1980	*Eight Plus One*
1983	*The Bumblebee Flies Anyway*
1985	*Beyond "The Chocolate War"*
1988	*Fade*

Other Novels

1960	*Now and the Hour*
1963	*A Little Raw On Monday Mornings*
1965	*Take Me Where the Good Times Are*

Chris Crutcher

I grew up in Cascade, Idaho, a small lumber and logging town of about 950 people in the mountains of west central Idaho, a town that later became (tavern for tavern, service station for service station, make-out spot for make-out spot) Trout, Idaho, in *Running Loose*. Not many people, least of all anyone connected with my education, would have—in their most psychotic moments—imagined I would ever write. My father was a smart and insightful man—for a Republican—who read voraciously and indiscriminately. He was a World War II B-17 pilot as conversant in the latest private eye novel as he was in the classics, as familiar with ancient biographies as popular fiction. He loved the act of reading, of gathering information. My mother was a "word" person who wrote poems for birthdays and anniversaries, played Scrabble with a vengeance, and corrected my grammar like a woman possessed.

My response to their appreciation of the written word was to read a grand total of one book from cover to cover during my entire four years of high school, opting rather to invent titles for book reports, as well as stories to go with them, and choosing the names of the authors from the pages of the Boise telephone directory. Obviously I got into this storytelling business out of a definite and specific need.

I think it is no coincidence that the one book I did read in high school was *To Kill a Mockingbird,* because fifteen years after I graduated from college, became semiliterate, and decided to become a storyteller, stories like Harper Lee's were the only kind I had any desire to tell: stories about real life as I see it, about my sense of justice and injustice.

Like all writers, my work is colored by the parts of life with which I've chosen to surround myself. I spent nearly ten years as director of a K–12 alternative school for kids who for one reason or another couldn't make it in the public school system, in inner-city Oakland, California. One More Last Chance High School in *The Crazy Horse Electric Game* was drawn directly from my experience there. I chose to leave urban America when I realized about a third of my life was being spent standing in line, so I headed back to the Northwest, where I had attended Eastern Washington State College fifteen years earlier, majoring in sociology and psychology. (In reality, and my grade point average bears this out, I majored in swimming.) In Spokane, Washington, I took a job as a child and family therapist in a mental health center, where I remain today, focusing on families involved in child abuse.

What I believe I have gained, and what I hope my writing reflects from working these past twenty years with people in difficult situations, is a sense of the connection between all human beings—the ghastly as well as the glorious, an awareness of the damage we do as a society creating unreal expectations for ourselves, and a different perspective on the true nature of courage. For me, those are things worth exploring and writing about.

Bibliography

1983   *Running Loose*
1986   *Stotan!*
1987   *The Crazy Horse Electric Game*
1988   *Chinese Handcuffs*

Maureen Daly

Yesterday, here in Palm Desert, California, where I now live, I was bitten by a chow dog. I had stopped at the home of a real estate agent to pick up a key to a vacant house I wanted to see and the dog slipped out the door and nipped me above the ankle right through my clean, white duck pants.

This was a black chow with a black mouth and tongue, but all chows have a tendency to bite when allowed.

The red chow of my childhood, named Kinkee because she had a kink in her arched, curled tail and because the name sounded Chinese, also had the characteristic black mouth and tongue of the chow world. But she was a house dog, walked on a leash and only allowed a good run on weekends and under supervision.

I have been writing and publishing since I was fifteen years old, and this is the first time I have ever mentioned that dog, Kinkee. This is renewed evidence to me that for most writers, nothing is wasted. Bits of fact, fancy, and "remembered fiction" are always tucked away in the computer brain, ready to take out as needed.

When Fond du Lac, Wisconsin, was a smaller town than it is today, my family lived at the eastern edge, the last house before the fields and creeks and empty spaces of Wisconsin set in. I had three sisters and a pair of good parents who brought their children to the United States from Castlecaufield, Ireland, and for years my family, the neat white house with the hedged gardens, the rough waters of Lake Winnebago a few blocks away, and those endless fields to play in, summer and winter—that was my whole life.

In those years I learned to love almost everything and to see and feel the things I began to write about. Such a simple childhood was an unsolicited gift.

61

We owned two special books in these early years, *The Burgess Book of Birds* and *The Burgess Book of Flowers*. We four sisters often took the Burgess books out to the fields in warm weather, lay in the tall grass, and tried to identify everything around us. There was much to see.

Besides those open fields, our parents "gave us" all the great, dangerous beauty of Lake Winnebago. We knew those waters from swimming, fishing, sailing, and ice-skating on winter's rough, frozen surfaces, always alert for the snap of ice, cracking and shifting from the pull of underground springs.

And my parents "gave us" the Fond du Lac public library, a grey stone building donated by Andrew Carnegie, with thousands of books and periodicals, and two magic librarians, Miss Jaynes and Miss Kramer. Each daughter had her personal library card and her personal bookshelves—fruit crates set on end in the corner of our bedrooms.

I published my first novel, *Seventeenth Summer,* and had my first bylined newspaper column in the *Chicago Tribune* while I was still in college. Since then, for dozens of years and a dozen countries of the world, with a family of my own creation, I have been writing both fact and fiction.

There is so much to want to say. The astonishment never ends. But it all began for me, the need to write, in the books and birds of Fond du Lac.

Bibliography

Books for Young Adults

1942	*Seventeenth Summer*
1944	*Smarter and Smoother*
1950	*Profile of Youth*
1958	*Mention My Name in Mombasa* (by William McGivern and Maureen Daly McGivern)
1960	*Spanish Roundabout*
1962	*Moroccan Roundabout*
1965	*Spain: Wonderland of Contrasts*
1968	*Sixteen and Other Stories*
1980	*The Seeing* (by William McGivern and Maureen Daly McGivern)
1986	*Acts of Love*
1989	*First a Dream*

Books for Younger Readers

Paula Danziger

PHOTO: BOB NEWEY

N onfiction has never been my favorite type of writing, especially when it's my own autobiography. I'm never sure of what to include, of what someone else wants to know. So what I've decided to do is run all of the facts together (sort of like a run-on sentence but more like a "run-on life"). Here goes . . . (with a lot of dots) . . .

Born August 18, 1944, in Washington, D.C. (my parents always said that they made sure that I was born there so that no state could disown me) . . . grew up in Virginia, Pennsylvania, and New Jersey . . . I have a younger brother . . . I've always loved books because they offered me a chance to escape from my real world and go into worlds that offered me more hope and more excitement . . . I've known since second grade that I wanted to be a writer . . . have always been fascinated with the infinite possibilities of what someone can do with the alphabet and imagination . . . I wrote for my high school newspaper and the local town paper . . . went to college, studied speech therapy, changed my major, didn't graduate on time because I flunked gym and earth science . . .

The most important thing that happened to me in college was that I met a poet named John Ciardi . . . he and his family became a very important part of my life and they took me to the Breadloaf Writer's Conference . . . I also spent a lot of time listening to what John had to say about writing and literature . . . When I finally graduated as an English major, I became a permanent substitute for six months (that sounds more like an unpermanent substitute), then was a Title I teacher for a year, and then taught junior high English . . . had two car accidents in six days (I didn't cause either of them) . . . as a result of the second accident hurt my head and had trouble reading and writing and had to quit teaching . . . It was a very scary, unhappy time in my life . . . I went back to college for a master's degree in reading, and started writing my first book . . . got my degree . . . the first book got accepted for publication (*The Cat Ate My Gymsuit*) . . . I wrote and had other jobs for about five years and then became a full-time writer . . .

I spend a lot of time traveling around the world, speaking to kids and adults about books and writing . . . I have no kids . . . I borrow them . . . I love to read, travel, be with friends, learn about new things . . .

Whew . . . that about covers it . . .

Actually, that just takes care of some of the facts. A limitation of five hundred words makes it hard to tell everything . . . as does my desire for privacy and for letting my books speak for themselves.

As much as I care about the written word, it is not easy to convey, on the page, who I am, so I hope that someday we can meet . . . at a school, at a conference, at a video arcade, in a library . . . Until then, let's all continue to read lots of books.

Bibliography

1974   *The Cat Ate My Gymsuit*
1978   *The Pistachio Prescription*
1979   *Can You Sue Your Parents for Malpractice?*
1980   *There's a Bat in Bunk Five*
1982   *The Divorce Express*
1985   *It's an Aardvark-Eat-Turtle World*
1986   *This Place Has No Atmosphere*
1987   *Remember Me to Harold Square*
1989   *Everyone Else's Parents Said Yes*

Lois Duncan

I can't remember a time when I didn't think of myself as a writer. When I was three years old I was dictating poems and stories to my parents, and as soon as I learned to print, I was writing them down for myself. At ten, I was submitting stories to magazines, and at thirteen I started selling them. Throughout my teens I wrote regularly for youth publications, such as *Seventeen*, and I wrote my first young adult novel when I was twenty.

Obviously, I was not your everyday, well-adjusted kid. A shy, homely little girl, I was a bookworm and a dreamer. My parents, Joseph and Lois Steinmetz, were magazine photographers, and we lived in Sarasota, Florida, where they were in a good position to take photo assignments throughout the southeast United States and the Caribbean. As a child, I spent a lot of time playing alone in the woods and on the beaches. I came out of my shell to some extent in high school, but was still a little strange, and probably still am. My autobiographical how-to book, *Chapters: My Growth as a Writer,* written for young people who want to become writers, describes those developmental years and includes some of the stories and poems I wrote during that time period.

Because I started writing so young, it was natural that my early books were for and about teenagers. After all, what else did I know about? Later, as the mother of five, I continued to write for young people. I kept a typewriter set up on the kitchen table and produced pages of manuscript between cooking meals and running loads of laundry. A major turning point in my life was when I was hired to teach for the journalism department at the University of New Mexico and actually got out of the house every day. Not having been to college myself, I started taking classes and graduated cum laude with a degree in English at age forty-two.

Today I live in Albuquerque, New Mexico, with my husband, Don Arquette, an electrical engineer, and the two of our children who are still at home. As for my writing career, I wear two hats. As a contributing editor for *Woman's Day* magazine, I travel on assignment and write nonfiction articles for adults. As an author of books for children and teenagers, I have the fun of creating characters and dreaming up adventures to send them on.

As with most fiction writers, bits and pieces of my own life are reflected in my stories. The beach house in *A Gift of Magic* is where I grew up. My hobby is photography, and the mother in *Summer of Fear* is a photographer. The psychopathic Mark, in *Killing Mr. Griffin*, was the boyfriend of one of my daughters (what a nightmare that was!). *The Twisted Window* is set in the mountains surrounding my home. Josie, in *Locked in Time*, is my youngest daughter, Kate, who had a difficult adolescence; the idea that life might magically flip into a holding pattern, trapping the two of us in our mother-daughter power struggle for all eternity, struck me as so horrible that I had to get a book out of it. I have recently become a grandmother, and my most recent project, *Songs from Dreamland,* is a book of original lullabies, packaged with a cassette of my musician daughter, Robin Arquette, singing them.

I feel very lucky to have known so early what I wanted from life and to have had that dream become reality.

Bibliography

Books for Young Adults

1958   *Debutante Hill*
1958   *Love Songs for Joyce* (written as Lois Kerry)
1959   *A Promise for Joyce* (written as Lois Kerry)
1960   *The Middle Sister*
1962   *Game of Danger*
1965   *Season of the Two-Heart*
1966   *Ransom*
1968   *They Never Came Home*
1970   *Peggy*
1971   *A Gift of Magic*
1973   *I Know What You Did Last Summer*
1974   *Down a Dark Hall*
1976   *Summer of Fear*

1976	*Killing Mr. Griffin*
1979	*Daughters of Eve*
1981	*Stranger with My Face*
1982	*Chapters: My Growth as a Writer*
1984	*The Third Eye*
1985	*Locked in Time*
1987	*The Twisted Window*
1989	*Don't Look Behind You*

Books for Younger Readers

1959	*The Littlest One in the Family*
1962	*Silly Mother*
1962	*Giving Away Suzanne*
1969	*Major Andre, Brave Enemy*
1971	*Hotel for Dogs*
1982	*From Spring to Spring*
1983	*The Terrible Tales of Happy Days School*
1986	*Horses of Dreamland*
1988	*Wonder Kid Meets the Evil Lunch Snatcher*
1989	*Songs from Dreamland*
1989	*The Birthday Moon*

Books for Adults

1966	*Point of Violence*
1974	*When the Bough Breaks*
1979	*How To Write and Sell Your Personal Experiences*

Audiocassettes

1986	*Songs from Dreamland* (sung by Robin Arquette)
1987	*Dream Songs from Yesterday* (sung by Robin Arquette)
1987	*Selling Personal Experiences to Magazines*
1988	*Our Beautiful Day* (sung by Robin Arquette)
1989	*The Story of Christmas* (sung by Robin Arquette)

Paula Fox

PHOTO: THOMAS VICTOR

I was born in New York City in 1923. When I was eight, I went to live on a Cuban plantation for two years, where I went to a one-room school with eight other students, who ranged in age from six to fourteen. This posed a classroom dilemma for the teacher, who was obliged to be very inventive to keep the youngest of us from falling asleep while the older children learned their arithmetic, and to stop the older ones from assaulting each other out of boredom while the youngest learned to read. After I left Cuba, I seldom lived any place longer than a year or so. I attended nine schools before I was twelve, by which time I had discovered that freedom, solace, and truth were to be found mostly in public libraries.

I wrote a detective story when I was seven. It was so bloody that, appalled by my own invention, I saw to it that various corpses were magically restored to life by the end of the story. I began to write—less luridly—when my sons were ten and twelve. My first book for children was *Maurice's Room*, the idea for which grew out of a conversation with a friend about the vast quantity of meaningless objects which surround middle-class children.

I taught school for a number of years after I returned from Europe, where I was a string girl for an English news service—a stringer was on the lowest rung of the journalistic ladder.

I have been writing steadily for a quarter of a century. Now and then, during that time, I have taught writing workshops at the University of Pennsylvania, and once at the State University of New York.

I write about what preoccupies me. I think a good deal about the passage from moral innocence to moral knowledge, and how, paradoxically, moral knowledge—almost always gained through suffering—is inextricably tangled with happiness.

But there is mystery in all stories, I believe, especially for the writers of them. That is one reason why it is so difficult to answer the question so often asked of writers, "Where do you get your ideas?"

The "idea," more often than not, is something discovered by the reader while the writer continues, through her books, to try to find the truth from which ideas spring.

Bibliography

Books for Young Adults

1970	*Blowfish Live in the Sea*
1974	*The Slave Dancer*
1980	*A Place Apart*
1984	*The Moonlight Man*
1986	*Lily and the Lost Boy*
1988	*The Village by the Sea*

Books for Younger Readers (selected)

1967	*How Many Miles to Babylon?*
1968	*The Stone-Faced Boy*
1968	*The Little Swineherd and Other Tales*
1970	*Portrait of Ivan*

Alan Garner

I was born in the front bedroom of 47 Crescent Road, Congleton, Cheshire, at 8:00 p.m., on Wednesday, 17 October 1934. My mother was a tailor, and my father a decorator.

My mother's family were cranks, and those who got away with it were respectable. Even the names are odd. There was a Great Aunt Sophia Pitchfork; and a great-grand-uncle, J. Sparkes Hall, was an inventor and is said to have designed the first elastic-sided boot. Another was a self-styled Professor of Systematic Memory or Polymnemonics. In the eighteenth century, the Halls tried to cover their traces, but documentary fragments and photographs suggest that a pawnbroker Hall of Plymouth had the fashionable tastes of the time, and so my great-great-great-great-grandmother may have been West African.

My father's family is quite different. They have been craftsmen, or at least skilled, for centuries. They have married locally, and have lived in the same house without a break of tenancy. My cousin lives there now. The house stands on the slopes of Alderley Edge, a wooded sandstone hill above the Cheshire Plain, and nearly all my books have been set in the landscape around this spot.

So there are three main elements in me from the start. Families on the one side gifted, unstable, and on the other, skilled, steady; and a hill that Garners have inhabited and worked under for as long as anybody knows.

I went to the local village school, and was taught by some of the teachers who had taught my father and uncles, so I got used to being called Harry, Syd, Dick, or Colin. The teachers' confusion was understandable, because I was hardly ever at school. I was spectacularly ill for most of the time, and childhood for me is memory of lying in bed and trying to will my pot to turn over. I'm sure I nearly succeeded twice. Twice, also, I heard the doctor and my family discuss my imminent death. They gave me up three times, but I remember hearing them only twice. The worst was when I had meningitis. I couldn't move, and they were talking about me as if I wasn't alive or real. I couldn't speak, but the fury should have blown the roof off. "How dare you?" I was screaming silently; and that's probably why I stayed alive.

Berserker rage is no blessing, and so I hardly ever allow myself to lose my temper. I was a physical coward at school, and had a lot of practice at running away. But I was the only one who could do Tarzan's war cry, and we adapted the Edge to our needs, with me a grounded ape man, because I was scared of climbing, and the baddies up in the trees.

Later, the natural instinct for cowardice became an athletic gift. From the age of twelve to eighteen I spent three hours a day running in an anti-clockwise direction in preparation for travelling several hundred miles in order to sprint a short distance as quickly as possible. Then, one day, the national coach said that, if all went well, I'd make an Olympic semifinal. I retired on the spot, out of respect for the man's accurate assessment.

But there was more to it than unwillingness to lose. I was forced to make two decisions, which eventually led me to write a book.

The first was that I had to question the value of an activity where success could be achieved only at the cost of other men's failure. The second was that I wanted the opposite to athletics, where it's all downhill to old age at thirty. I realised that I wanted to live actively for as long as possible and to go out on a crescendo; which meant that I should always be striving, failing, developing: a donkey that must never catch the carrot.

Two compulsory years in the army gave the feelings room to grow, and by the time I went to Oxford University I knew that I was heading in the wrong direction. It was a negative state to be in, and only by eliminating what I found unpalatable was I able to arrive at a way out. I was sitting on a tree stump, waiting for a bus, when everything became simple. The answer to my problems was to be a writer. Material needs were warmth and food. All else beyond that point, whether a pencil sharpener or an ocean-going yacht, was a luxury.

I left Oxford, looked for—and found—my present house, dug myself in, and wrote. I was twenty-two years old.

And that is how it has gone on. I am a writer. I write for myself and for no other audience. Yet, for some reason that I do not understand, I am read with far greater passion, intelligence, and commitment by young people than by adults. Is that strange?

Bibliography

Books for Young Adults and Adults

1960   *The Weirdstone of Brisingamen. A Tale of Alderley* (in America as *The Weirdstone: A Tale of Alderley*)

1963   *The Moon of Gomrath*

1965   *Elidor*

1967   *The Owl Service*

1969   *The Hamish Hamilton Book of Goblins* (editor), illus. by Krystyna Turska (in U.S. as *A Cavalcade of Goblins*)

1970   *The Old Man of Mow*, photographs by Roger Hill

1973   *Red Shift*

1975   *The Guizer: A Book of Fools*, with illus. by V. Pritchard

1975   *The Breadhorse*, illus. by Albin Trowski

1976   *The Stone Book*, illus. by Michael Foreman

1977   *Tom Fobble's Day*, illus. by Michael Foreman

1977   *Granny Reardun*, illus. by Michael Foreman

1978   *The Aimer Gate*, illus. by Michael Foreman

1979   *The Girl of the Golden Gate; The Golden Brothers; The Princess and the Golden Mane; The Three Golden Heads of the Well*, illus. by Michael Foreman (in one volume as *Alan Garner's Fairytales of Gold*)

1980   *The Lad of the Gad*

Other Works

1966   *Holly from the Bongs, A Nativity Play*, photographs by Roger Hill, music by William Mayne

1974   *Holly from the Bongs, A Nativity Opera*, music by Gordon Crosse

1975   *Potter Thompson*, music by Gordon Crosse

Jean Craighead George

My African gray parrot is sitting on my shoulder saying, "Mother, are you all right?" Qimmiq, my Alaskan malamute, is outside greeting the dawn with a wolf howl. And a large-mouthed bass in the pool in my foyer is churning the water to tell me it's time to feed him. My granddaughters, Rebecca and Katie, have come downstairs to listen in amazement to the parrot speaking English. In this atmosphere I write best—a housescape in which there are children and wild things around me.

As the daughter of two naturalist-entomologists and the sister of identical twin brothers who have become experts on the grizzly bears of Wyoming, I grew up in a household just like the above. In our Washington, D.C., home there were falcons, owls, bombardier beetles, and lizards inside and outside. John and Frank, my brothers, and I studied our lessons with opossums on our laps and barn owls coming in and out of the windows. We spent weekends following our parents along the Potomac River bottomlands learning the plants and animals or sitting for hours watching a spider weave an orb web.

After each weekend, I would come home and write. At first I wrote poetry. I was in the third grade, full of the love of nature and words, but unable to sit still very long. Poems could be short, so I wrote poems about everything I saw: a toad under a stone, a piece of coal in the basement.

My ability to write longer works improved as I developed discipline and expanded my reading. In junior high school I went from poems to epic poems to short stories. In college I attempted the essay; after college I became a journalist for the *Washington Post;* and, finally at the age of twenty-four, I took on the novel. I have been writing novels for young people ever since, almost all of them about characters learning about themselves from nature.

Over the forty years I have been writing, I have never lost the need to be surrounded by beautiful birds and beasts and the hills and valleys that inspired my first poems. To do this, I hike, canoe, and camp out under the stars. I keep baby raccoons, lost birds, toads, and bullfrogs in and outside my home. And to fulfill my need to have children around, I import my granddaughters from Baltimore or my grandnephews from across the Hudson River.

I also will not write what I have not seen or experienced. To do this I travel to wild and inspiring places. Several years ago, Craig, one of my three children, invited me to join his group of scientists and Eskimos studying bowhead whales from a camp on the Arctic ice. When I arrived in that vast whiteness it was April and thirty-five degrees below zero. I was given warm clothing and a few warnings about the ice breaking and a floe carrying me off to Siberia. I was also given a rifle and instructed not to leave camp without it. "Polar bears," my son said, "are hungry this time of year. They will attack people." Nonsense, I thought, but picked up my gun whenever I went out to watch the behemoth whales swim past our camp.

One morning a young scientist was sitting in the warm cook tent when he heard someone unzipping the flaps. He looked up to see a huge white paw with long black claws opening the zipper . . . As I wrote *Water Sky,* a book about a bowhead whale and the Eskimos, the story of the attacking polar bear worked its way into the pages, along with the treacherous ice, the cold, and the gorgeous land of the midnight sun.

Then I traveled south. Two years ago, I camped on a desert island off the coast of Baja, Mexico, with my youngest son, Luke, an ornithologist. While I was snorkling to learn the names and behavior of the reef fish, an enormous hammerhead shark, known to have killed humans, slithered past me. That incident contributed to *Shark Beneath the Reef.*

I always come home to write. I need my special world of Tocca the parrot talking to me, Qimmiq howling to the wind, and, if possible, Katie and Rebecca running in and out my patio door, just as their mother and her brothers did years ago.

Bibliography

Books for Children and Young Adults

1948   *Vulpes the Red Fox*
1949   *Vison the Mink*
1950   *Masked Prowler, The Story of a Raccoon*
1952   *Meph the Pet Skunk*
1954   *Bubo the Great Horned Owl*
1956   *Dipper of Copper Creek*
1957   *Hole in the Tree*
1958   *Snow Tracks*
1959   *My Side of the Mountain*
1962   *The Summer of the Falcon*
1963   *Red Robin Fly Up!*
1964   *Gull Number 737*
1966   *Hold Zero*
1968   *Coyote in Manhattan*
1970   *Beastly Inventions: A Surprising Investigation into How Smart Animals Really Are*
1971   *All Upon a Stone*
1971   *Who Really Killed Cock Robin?*
1972   *Julie of the Wolves*
1972   *Everglades Wildguide*
1974   *All Upon a Sidewalk*
1975   *Hook a Fish, Catch a Mountain*
1976   *Going to the Sun*
1977   *The Wentletrap Trap*
1977   *The American Walk Book*
1978   *The Wounded Wolf*
1979   *River Rats*
1982   *Journey Inward* (autobiography)
1982   *The Wild, Wild Cookbook*
1982   *The Grizzly Bear with the Golden Ears*
1983   *The Talking Earth*
1986   *How to Talk to Your Animals*
1987   *Water Sky*
1989   *Shark Beneath the Reef*
1989   *On the Far Side of the Mountain*

Series

1967–69   *The Thirteen Moons*
1983–87   *One Day in the ... [Desert, Alpine Tundra, Prairie, Woods]*

Barbara Girion

I would like to be able to report that I fell out of my crib and immediately started writing, but that wouldn't be true. I grew up and went to school in Hillside, New Jersey, and while I loved books and loved to read, I hated to write, especially essays or reports—e.g., "What I Did on My Summer Vacation"—that were assigned by teachers.

I worked after school in my father's 5 & 10 cent store, teased my younger brother, and was a gung-ho cheerleader in my high school years. Still, my favorite place was always the library, and I once tried, like my favorite heroine, Francie Nolan in *A Tree Grows in Brooklyn*, to read through all the books alphabetically.

After graduating from college, where I majored in history, I married and got a job teaching seventh grade in the very same school that I had attended in Hillside, New Jersey. It was eerie walking through the halls that had somehow gotten so much smaller over the years and going into the Teachers Room (where I finally learned that teachers really didn't have such secret things to talk about!).

When my first son was born, I found it impossible to get him to take a nap unless I told him a story. So I'd stretch out on the couch and begin to weave tales about the everyday things around us. I don't know if the stories were boring or my voice was, but he'd soon be asleep. It was faster than rocking him in his carriage. But I'd be wide awake and my mind would keep on with the stories. The hardest decision I've ever had to make took place on the day I decided to get these stories out of my head and onto a piece of paper.

I soon realized that I could recall all the feelings I had growing up. The happiness, the sadness, the fears and the triumphs. After my second son and daughter came along and I was able to borrow Grandma and Grandpa to babysit, I signed up for a writers' workshop in New York City.

That became the highlight of a busy mother's week. On Wednesday nights I'd travel to class, clutching my typewritten pages, heart beating madly. I'd either wind up crying all the way back home to New Jersey if my work was heavily criticized or be wildly happy if I had received some compliments.

I've never had the desire to write fantasy. I guess I'm too fascinated by the real people and happenings that surround me. All of my work so far is contemporary in nature, though the feelings my characters have are the same feelings I had growing up and I daresay the same feelings young people will have fifty years from now. Since my personal family background is a very strong one, I like to use the generations of families in my books. I had loving and interested grandparents. Although immigrants themselves, they impressed upon me the love and reverence for books that I try to pass on to my own children.

From my own experience as a parent, I know that parents are neither heroes nor the completely selfish, coldblooded devils that they are made out to be. I am not trying to write about the family extremes, the abusers or the staunchest, most wonderful. Somehow, I am trying to write about those of us who muddle through, who make mistakes at times but are still around with an awful lot of love to give.

I try to learn from each of my books. They are almost like my children. I try to put the very best of myself into them that I can. Then I send them out into the world, where they have to stand or fall by themselves.

Bibliography

Books for Young Adults

1979	*A Tangle of Roots*
1981	*A Handful of Stars*
1983	*In the Middle of a Rainbow*
1984	*A Very Brief Season* (short stories)

Books for Younger Readers

| 1978 | *The Boy with the Special Face* |

Series

Bette Greene

PHOTO: RICHARD MacLEOD

I grew up on a dry, dusty speck of earth known as Parkin, Arkansas, a town so small that everybody not only knew everybody else, but knew each other's secrets too. And it was certainly no secret that a lot of townspeople did a lot of praying for me because they were convinced that my soul would sizzle and crackle in the hottest pits of Hell because my family and I were Jewish rather than Baptist like everybody else. At the time, I felt intensely disloyal to my parents because in my own secret heart of hearts I wanted to be Baptist and really belong. And by the way, bypassing Hell would also have to be considered a big—a very big—plus.

Well, that was an awful lot of years ago, and I've stopped worrying about either belonging or the state of my soul, but I haven't stopped worrying (and writing about) people who are bigoted towards everybody else's religion because they're convinced beyond rhyme or reason that God is so exclusive that he only whispers in their ears.

Back in Parkin I had two great ambitions. First, because I clerked in my parents' dry goods store, I wanted to be the world's greatest salesperson, certain that would help my mother and father forget what a terrible student I was. And second, I wanted *not* to be humiliated by missing the very first word at our school's annual spelling bee. Of course, my folks never for a moment forgot what a terrible student I was, *and* I did misspell the first word, the very first word.

Many years later when I was studying writing at Columbia University, I traded in those two failed ambitions for still another ambition. This time I was determined to write a book so real, so intensely emotional that every single reader would be compelled to see what I saw and feel what I felt.

Bibliography

1973   *Summer of My German Soldier*
1974   *Philip Hall Likes Me, I Reckon Maybe*
1978   *Morning Is a Long Time Coming*
1981   *Get on Out of Here, Philip Hall*
1983   *Them That Glitter and Them That Don't*
1990   *The Drowning of Stephan Jones*

Constance C. Greene

I am a native New Yorker and have used the city as background for some of my books, notably the Al series, as well as *I and Sproggy.* My father, grandfather, and mother were all newspaper people. The printed word was very much a part of my life and still is. I graduated from Marymount School in New York and attended Skidmore College for two years, after which I worked for the Associated Press in New York. All the young men were at war and I worked nights in the mailroom for $16.50 a week. In time I was promoted to the city desk and interviewed Frank Sinatra, Marlene Dietrich, and Lady Astor. Plus I went to Staten Island to greet troopships full of returning soldiers.

It was first class training for a writer, I discovered. Working for a wire service meant a few words had to do the work of many. That was important knowledge for me. As a result, I write tight and seldom have to cut.

In 1946 I married Philip Greene and had five children in seven years. My first book, *A Girl Called Al,* is dedicated to them. Children are work, and writing is work, and seldom the twain shall meet. When my children were small I wrote short stories, my favorite literary form. I had never thought of writing for children. When my youngest child went off to kindergarten I joined a writer's workshop in Connecticut, where we lived then. It was a wonderful experience. I'm not sure that without it I could've gone on. The people in the workshop were hard-working and dedicated, and we were all in the same boat: aspiring writers longing to be published.

Then along came Al, purely a figment of my imagination. I wanted to write about a city kid, as that was what I had been.

"You have the bones, now flesh them out," the editor at Viking told me. I did as she advised me to do and I've been writing children's books ever since. My books are for kids ages eight through twelve. Middle-aged kids. This is not by design but because these are my favorite ages. Kids are so open at that age, so unself-conscious, so completely themselves. I write to entertain, not to educate. I hope I never preach to them. I try not to.

I have written two young adult books for ages twelve and up for Harper and Row. My other books have all been published by Viking. The YAs are tougher for me to write. I'm ambivalent about the category. Ideally, it seems to me that kids past twelve should be exploring adult literature, as well as books that excited or thrilled or comforted them when they were little. At twelve, the sky's the limit.

A writer is almost always asked where his or her ideas come from. I am just putting the finishing touches on a sixth Al book, *Al's Blind Date.* I read a newspaper story about blind dates coming back into fashion. That did it. Blind dates are an interesting phenomenon and one Al and her friends are fascinated by. There is the idea. The execution of same is harder. Then I will do another YA for Harper. It will be about a boy named Virgil.

My son-in-law gave me the idea for *Double-Dare O'Toole,* about a boy named Fex O'Toole who finds it impossible to resist a double dare. *The Love Letters of J. Timothy Owen,* a YA, is about a boy who is shy and wants to get to know a girl better, so he copies some of the world's best love letters and sends them to her anonymously. This seemed to me a good idea. I'm all for more romance for the young, as well as writing love letters. I found the perfect book, one my husband had bought during the war, filled with love letters written by such as Franz Liszt, Admiral Lord Nelson, and Benjamin Franklin. Written in wonderfully flowery language, they were per-fect for my purpose.

My personal favorites are the Al books, especially the first, because it was the first, and *Beat the Turtle Drum.* This is the most autobiographical of all my books. It's about two sisters, one of whom dies. When I was eleven, my thirteen-year-old sister died. I wrote it to jog my memory. It happened a long time ago. The one certain thing is that the child dies. The rest is made up, except for the horse Joss rents with money saved from birthday presents. This was lifted from real life. All of my books combine the real and the made-up. Some children are bothered by the ending of *Beat the Turtle Drum* and have asked me to write a sequel. This I will never do. The first was difficult, the second impossible. I tell them, "Write your own sequel." And if you do, let me see it. I would like to know how it turns out. So far, no takers.

"Are you still writing?" people ask in a slightly jocular tone, as if writing were some sort of aberration.

"Are you still breathing?" I could reply rudely, and do not.

Once started, it's tough to stop.

Writing for children is quite lovely, the most rewarding career I can imagine. I feel fortunate it turned out to be the thing I do best.

Bibliography

Books for Children and Young Adults

1969	*A Girl Called Al*
1970	*Leo the Lioness*
1971	*The Good Luck Bogie Hat*
1972	*The Unmaking of Rabbit*
1973	*Isabelle the Itch*
1974	*The Ears of Louis*
1975	*I Know You, Al*
1976	*Beat the Turtle Drum*
1977	*Getting Nowhere*
1978	*I and Sproggy*
1979	*Your Old Pal, Al*
1980	*Dotty's Suitcase*
1981	*Double-Dare O'Toole*
1982	*Al(exandra) the Great*
1983	*Ask Anybody*
1984	*Isabelle Shows Her Stuff*
1985	*Star Shine*
1986	*Just Plain Al*
1986	*The Love Letters of J. Timothy Owen*
1988	*Monday I Love You*
1988	*Isabelle and Little Orphan Frannie*
1989	*Al's Blind Date*

Books for Adults

1985	*Other Plans*

Rosa Guy

My first choice of artistic expression was the theater. I joined the American Negro Theater to study. I soon learned the limitations for advancement of the black artist on the American scene—limitations caused by the overwhelming prejudice in the society against the color of one's skin. This prejudice limits black actors and actresses to the most peripheral roles in theater in the United States and in American-influenced theater throughout the world. Many of the greatest black performers I have known have had to be satisfied with depicting servants, prostitutes, or slaves—and this after years of study. The few who have gone on to recognition have never had the chance to be considered truly great. No Laurence Olivier, Spencer Tracy, or Ronald Coleman. Never did our actresses become the grande dames of stage-screen-television as did Helen Hayes, Katharine Hepburn, Ingrid Bergman, or Joan Crawford. The answer has always been "There are no works yet written." And yet black life pulses with energy and drama.

I came to the United States as a child of seven, and was orphaned at a young age, and so spent many of my growing years on the streets of New York. Before my eyes many dramas unfolded, dramas which out-Dickensed Dickens, and equaled if not rivaled the Brontë sisters in passion. Dramas to raise the consciousness of the truly committed: patterns of pride and prejudice, legends of the innocent and the damned, the intense struggles for human dignity—and survival. . . .

I was already married and had a son when the obvious flaw woven into the fabric of this democratic society drove me to turn my talents to writing. *Bird at My Window,* my first novel, was published over twenty years ago. My works are published all over the

85

world. Books of mine are a part of the syllabus in Great Britain. Today I look at those black artists who appear on stage, screen, and television. I look particularly for those who have been given roles depicting the lives of black folks—roles that have given them recognition as the grand talents on the American scene . . . and I keep on writing. . . .

Bibliography

1966   *Bird at My Window*
1969   *Children of Longing*
1973   *The Friends*
1976   *Ruby*
1978   *Edith Jackson*
1979   *The Disappearance*
1981   *Mirror of Her Own*
1981   *Mother Crocodile*
1983   *New Guys Around the Block*
1983   *A Measure of Time*
1984   *Paris, Pee Wee and Big Dog*
1985   *My Love, My Love, or the Peasant Girl*
1987   *And I Heard a Bird Sing*
1989   *The Ups and Downs of Carl Davis the Third*

Lynn Hall

My love for books began as soon as I was old enough to know that ponies existed . . . and I couldn't have one. Much of my childhood was spent in a solitary pursuit of that fictional world where girls who wanted horses got them.

In fact I thought it was terribly unfair of Velvet Brown to inherit *five* horses, and to win the Pi in the village lottery on top of it. Why should she have six when I didn't have any?

I grew up in Midwest suburbs, the middle of three daughters in a middle-middle-class family. My father owned a Standard Oil bulk plant and tank wagon service in a small suburb of Des Moines. Mother had been an English teacher and went back to teaching after her chicks had flown the coop.

Our father was a very good, decent man—hard-working, religious, and absolutely respected by everyone who knew him—but he was of the generation of men who had great difficulty expressing affection. Both of my sisters compensated by going into high school marriages.

I disappeared into my books and my dreams. The most constant dream was of a little house in the country, with horses and dogs, with fine music and quiet and solitude.

I, too, went into an unwise marriage but backed out of it almost immediately. My instincts warned me that this wasn't right for me.

In my mid-twenties, after several years of unsatisfying interim jobs, I began to consider the possibility of writing as a career. The major hurdle was in bridging the chasm between my self-image as a non–college person and my unrealistically elevated conception of writers as creative geniuses who sat at the right hand of God, so to speak.

But once the idea took root and began to grow, I became convinced that writing, and specifically writing the kind of animal books I'd always loved, was the best possible route to the life I wanted. I set a series of practical goals for myself: write a mid-grade dog story; write a book good enough to get published; find a publisher and write enough books to make a subsistence country-home living from the books alone.

I was prepared to spend many years just on the first few phases of the plan, but in fact it didn't take that long. I studied and analyzed armloads of dog and horse books from the library. I sold my chinchilla herd to finance six months of unemployment, during which I wrote my first two books. Within a year the first book was sold, and four years later I was able to kick free from my city existence and the ad agency copywriting job, and to head for the country.

That was twenty years and seventy books ago.

I lived happily ever after.

Bibliography

Books for Young Adults

1970	*Too Near the Sun*
1970	*Gently Touch the Milkweed*
1972	*Sticks and Stones*
1972	*The Seige of Silent Henry*
1976	*Flowers of Anger*
1980	*The Leaving*
1980	*The Horse Trader*
1981	*Danza!*
1981	*Tin Can Tucker*
1982	*Half the Battle*
1983	*Denison's Daughter*
1984	*Uphill All the Way*
1985	*The Giver*
1985	*Just One Friend*
1986	*If Winter Comes*
1986	*The Solitary*
1987	*Letting Go*

1987	*Flyaway*
1987	*Ride a Dark Horse*
1988	*Where Have All the Tigers Gone?*
1988	*A Killing Freeze*

Books for Younger Readers (selected)

1967	*The Shy Ones*
1968	*The Secret of Stonehouse*
1969	*Ride a Wild Dream*
1971	*A Horse Called Dragon*
1972	*Lynn Hall's Dog Stories*
1973	*Flash, Dog of Old Egypt*
1974	*Troublemaker*
1975	*Kids and Dog Shows*
1977	*Dragon the Defiant*
1978	*Careers for Dog Lovers*
1978	*The Mystery of Pony Hollow*
1980	*Mystery of the Plum Park Pony*
1980	*The Disappearing Grandad*
1982	*Megan's Mare*
1985	*Tazo and Me*
1986	*Danger Dog*
1988	*In Trouble Again, Zelda Hammersmith*
1988	*The Secret Life of Dagmar Schultz*
1989	*Here Comes Zelda Claus*

Virginia Hamilton

I grew up with four older brothers and sisters on a small farm in Yellow Springs, Ohio, a village that had been a station on the Underground Railroad and was the home of descendants of fugitive slaves. My mother, in fact, was the oldest daughter of a fugitive slave. My charming but moody father, a superb mandolinist, had run gambling halls in mining towns. During the depressed thirties when I was born, my parents turned the rich soil of our Miami Valley land into a productive farm, with enough left over to sell to a local grocery. After leaving home and living in New York City for fifteen years, I returned to live in the village of my childhood, where I raised two children with my husband, poet Arnold Adoff.

Being the "baby" of the family, I was given the freedom to discover whatever there was to find. My most important discovery was the rich storytelling abilities of my relatives—aunts, uncles, cousins, my mother's Perry clan, and my father, Ken Hamilton. When they weren't working the fields, they filled the air with stories and gossip and tall tales. And when they couldn't remember the details of the real events, they substituted their own imaginative fictions. They thus created and recreated who they were and where they had come from and what they hoped to be.

So it is perfectly natural that telling stories and retelling folktales is what I do best. And although I write realistic fiction—as I have done in *M.C. Higgins, the Great* and *A White Romance*—there is a great deal of fantasy and folklore in what I write—as there is, for example, in the *Justice* cycle as well as in *The Magical Adventures of Pretty Pearl.*

Race, too, is an important element in my books, though I don't sit down at my typewriter determined to write a Black story. It just happens that I know Black people better than I know any other kind of people because I am Black and I am comfortable writing about the people I know best. But more than anything, I write about emotions and themes which are common to all people: family unity, friendships, the importance of individual freedom, and the influence of our past heritage on the present. My aim is always to tell a good story.

The influence of the past is most evident in my first novel, *Zeeley,* and in biographies I've written on the writer W.E.B. DuBois and on the slave Anthony Burns, as well as in the folktales and stories I've retold in *The People Could Fly* and most recently in *In the Beginning: Creation Stories from Around the World.*

Contrary to what some people think, writing is hard labor. Although ideas seem to come to me out of nowhere—a glimpse, an image, a surprise thought—I have to chase after them to see where they are going. I have to follow a character to see how that individual interacts with friends, family, and neighbors. And I need to work with my hands, to type the words, not just to hear the words but to see the designs those words make on the paper. Thus I enjoy the typing and the revising. The rewriting process, in fact, is the activity that appeals to me most, for it is in the first and second revisions that the language of the initial creation begins to reveal its originality. Writing is physical labor, and I am not content until the book is published and I know that the labor is finished.

Language is magic to me, and words make worlds that others can understand. I am a believer in language and its magic monarchy.

Bibliography

Books for Young Adults

1967   *Zeeley*
1968   *The House of Dies Drear*
1971   *The Planet of Junior Brown*
1972   *W.E.B. DuBois: A Biography*
1974   *M.C. Higgins, the Great*
1974   *Paul Robeson: The Life and Times of a Free Black Man*
1976   *Arilla Sundown*
1976   *Illusion and Reality*
1978   *Justice and Her Brothers*

1980	*Dustland*
1980	*The Gathering*
1982	*Sweet Whispers, Brother Rush*
1984	*A Little Love*
1985	*Junius over Far*
1987	*The Mystery of Drear House*
1987	*A White Romance*
1988	*Anthony Burns: The Defeat and Triumph of a Fugitive Slave*

Books for Younger Readers

1969	*The Time-Ago Tales of Jadhu*
1973	*Time-Ago Lost: More Tales of Jadhu*
1980	*Jadhu*
1983	*Willie Bea and the Time the Martians Landed*
1984	*The Magical Adventures of Pretty Pearl*

Books for Readers of All Ages

1985	*The People Could Fly: American Black Folktales*
1988	*In the Beginning: Creation Stories from Around the World*, illus. by Barry Moser

Nat Hentoff

I was born in Boston, Massachusetts, on June 10, 1925. My primary formative influences were (1) being Jewish (a sense of social justice and also a strong sense of what it is to be hated as a group); (2) jazz (the freedom and risk-taking in the music and musicians and the direct emotion—in which there is no room for the player or the listener to hide); and (3) Boston Latin School (the oldest public school in America, where the faculty has high expectations of every student and will give no student an excuse not to meet those expectations).

In Boston, I was graduated, after Latin School, from Northeastern University, a working-class college. I then worked in radio (sports, news, jazz) for nine years; went to New York to be an editor of *Down Beat*, the jazz magazine; and then freelanced, writing not only about jazz but also about civil liberties (especially freedom of speech and privacy), education, civil rights, and politics.

Since 1958, I have been a weekly columnist for the *Village Voice* in New York; and since 1960, I have been a staff writer for *The New Yorker.* I also write a weekly column for the *Washington Post*, which is then syndicated nationally by the Copley News Service.

I started writing books for young adults at the suggestion of Ursula Nordstrom, who headed that department for a long time at Harper and Row. I was reluctant, not wanting to censor myself as to themes or language because of a young adult audience. She told me just to write a story, and not to worry about anything else. That first novel was *Jazz Country*, which was intended to give young black readers pride in their musical heritage and to show young white readers what it takes in character as well as skills to become a successful jazz musician.

93

A public librarian once gave me the compliment about my writing that I have most prized when she said about *Jazz Country*, "It's the book that is most often stolen from our shelves."

In recent years, I have worked with George Nicholson, editor-in-chief of books for young readers at Delacorte Press. He is an editor of extraordinary value because he has an aversion to stereotypes of all kinds, thereby encouraging his authors to try to be as imaginative as kids are.

Having written a good many books for adults, I particularly enjoy the responses of young readers, who write to authors far more often than adults, and often quite trenchantly. I fall behind in all the rest of my correspondence, but my ironclad rule is that a letter from a kid gets answered—right away. If there is a heaven, that might get me a shot at the waiting list.

Bibliography

Books for Young Adults

1965   *Jazz Country*
1968   *I'm Really Dragged But Nothing Gets Me Down*
1968   *Journey into Jazz*
1971   *In the Country of Ourselves*
1976   *This School Is Driving Me Crazy*
1981   *Does This School Have Capital Punishment?*
1982   *The Day They Came to Arrest the Book*
1987   *American Heroes: In and Out of School*

Nonfiction (selected)

1960   *Jazz Street*
1962   *The Jazz Life*
1966   *Our Children Are Dying*
1968   *A Doctor Among the Addicts*
1978   *Jazz Is*
1980   *The First Freedom: A Tumultuous History of Free Speech in America*
1986   *Boston Boy* (memoir)

Other Books

1967   *Journey into Jazz: For Narrator, Jazz Ensemble, and Small Orchestra* (narration, with music by Gunther Schuller)

S. E. Hinton

PHOTO: DAVID INHOFE

I was born in Tulsa, Oklahoma, and have lived there most of my life—three years in northern California and six months in Spain, the rest in Tulsa. I had a "normal" childhood, with parents, a younger sister, cousins, aunts, uncles, grandparents, dogs, cats, etc. (although I had to wait until I was grown to get my first horse). I was a tomboy, played football, hunted; most of my close friends were boys, which probably accounts for my use of a male narrator.

I wrote *The Outsiders* when I was sixteen years old. It was the third book I'd written, but the first I tried to get published. I'd been writing—short stories, journals, poetry—for many years. Most writers get into writing as sheer self-indulgence. Nobody would do it unless they liked to. It's hard enough if you like to.

I'd always liked to read (and still do, almost compulsively). By sixteen I had read so much that things like sentence structure, paragraphing, and pacing were in my subconscious. I only had to worry about my story.

When I was sixteen there was no "young adult" literature. If you were through with the horse books and not ready for adult books there wasn't much to read except *Mary Jane Goes to the Prom*, and I couldn't stand to read that stuff. So I wrote *The Outsiders* partly because I wanted something realistic to read that dealt with teenagers.

I was fortunate to hit on a universal theme—the "In" group versus the "Out" group, which is one reason why the book is still being read today. The labels may change, but the groups go on forever. I also wrote it at the right time. The emotions in *The Outsiders,* strong as they are, are the true emotions of a teenager.

I have kept on writing about teenagers because, unlike most adults, I like them. It's an interesting time of life, chockfull of dramatic possibilities.

I met my husband when seated next to him in Freshman Biology (appropriately) and married him four years later. Five years ago we had a baby, as we desperately needed something new to talk about.

My favorite pastimes (besides reading) are horseback riding (I show hunters), swimming, and taking long walks—fun things to do with others, but just as fun alone.

Because I've worked on three out of four of the movies of my books, people assume there is something glamorous about my life, which is not the case. The movies were hard work and a lot of fun, but they didn't take up much of my life. Wandering around the Safeway, wondering what to cook for dinner—*that* takes up much of my life.

I like cats, lemons, looking at views. I don't like sweets, games, TV, giving speeches, air travel, or *writing about myself.* Unfortunately, the last three seem to be included in the job. When I got started I thought all a novelist had to do was write novels. But I was young . . .

My favorite reading includes a lot of history and biography. My favorite novels are *Fire from Heaven* by Mary Renault, *Kristin Lavransdatter* by Sigrid Undset, *Emma* by Jane Austen, and *The Haunting of Hill House* by Shirley Jackson. Now that I look at this list I realize that all are character studies. And it's obvious that I read better than I write.

There isn't much else to say, since I strongly believe writing is something you do, not something you talk about.

Bibliography

1967	*The Outsiders*
1971	*That Was Then, This Is Now*
1975	*Rumble Fish*
1979	*Tex*
1988	*Taming the Star Runner*

Isabelle Holland

I think of myself as a storyteller and for this I am indebted to my mother. As the child of a Foreign Service officer, I was born and brought up abroad—Switzerland, Guatemala, and England—and Mother's mode of keeping me entertained was to tell me stories, wonderful tales beginning, "Once upon a time. . . ."

As the years passed and I got older and started reading for myself, I found many of these stories in history, legend, the Bible, and novels. But at the time my mother told them, they came to me as exciting tales made up for me at that moment. This left me with the firm view that stories, however long—and this includes those of the length of *War and Peace*—should above all be interesting.

I sold my first story when I was thirteen to an English children's magazine called *Tiger Tim*. Always attracted to the thought of reward, I responded to an invitation in the magazine which said, "Write us a story of three hundred words. If we publish it we will send you a prize." So I wrote *Naughty Betty*, about a little girl who hated to practice the piano, because I hated to practice the piano, and sent if off. It was published and I got my prize, a book (what better?).

This triumph was followed by years and years of trying to write another *Gone With the Wind* about a riverboat gambler on the Mississippi who lost everything gambling in a dive in New Orleans. My hero is still in that French Quarter dive! I could never figure out how to get him out! Foreseeing the end of a plot was always a difficulty until I learned that if I just kept on going, no matter what, the ending would come of its own logic.

My first book, *Cecily*, was published in 1967. *Cecily* was a semi-autobiographical story about a fat, miserable thirteen-year-old in an English boarding school where the ideal was to be tall, blond, flat-chested, and good at games. If published today, *Cecily* would undoubtedly be brought out by the young adult department of the publisher. But at that time, young adult books, as a separate category, were a new concept, so *Cecily* appeared on the adult list.

The Man Without a Face, my first young adult novel, was actually my third book to be published and was written when I had become a freelance writer. The others followed, interspersed by children's and adult books. In *Of Love and Death and Other Journeys,* I used my summers in Umbria in Italy. In *Heads You Win, Tails I Lose,* I dealt with the problem common to so many adolescent girls (myself included) of losing weight. Some of my later books for young adults have been written in the form of mysteries—a form I love to read and also write because it still adheres to the old discipline of a beginning, a middle, an end, and a resolution. But all my books, whatever the category or form, deal, most importantly, with the inner journey of the central character.

By the end of 1989 I will have had published forty-three, possibly forty-four, books, thirteen of them for young adults.

What are the most important things I have learned about the craft of writing? There are two: First, write as near every day as possible. Second, whatever happens, go on!

Bibliography

Books for Young Adults

1972	*The Man Without a Face*
1973	*Heads You Win, Tails I Lose*
1975	*Of Love and Death and Other Journeys*
1977	*Hitchhike*
1981	*Summer of My First Love*
1983	*Perdita*
1983	*The Empty House*
1983	*After the First Love*
1984	*The Island*
1985	*Jenny Kiss'd Me*
1987	*Love and the Genetic Factor*
1987	*Toby the Splendid*
1989	*Thief*
1989	*The Unfrightening Dark*

Books for Children

1970	*Amanda's Choice*
1972	*The Mystery of Castle Rinaldi*
1974	*Journey for Three*
1977	*Alan and the Animal Kingdom*
1978	*Dinah and the Green Fat Kingdom*
1980	*Now Is Not Too Late*
1982	*A Horse Named Peaceable*
1982	*Abbie's God Book*
1983	*God, Mrs. Muskrat and Aunt Dot*
1984	*Green Andrew Green*
1984	*Kevin's Hat*
1986	*Henry and Grudge*
1987	*The Christmas Cat*
1989	*The Easter Donkey*

Books for Adults

1967	*Cecily*
1974	*Kilgaren*
1974	*Trelawny*
1975	*Moncrieff*
1976	*Darcourt*
1976	*Grenelle*
1977	*The deMaury Papers*
1978	*Tower Abbey*
1979	*The Marchington Inheritance*
1980	*Counterpoint*
1981	*The Lost Madonna*
1984	*A Death at St. Anselm's*
1985	*Flight of the Archangel*
1986	*A Lover Scorned*
1988	*Bump in the Night*

Helen Mary (H. M.) Hoover

I t is rare now for children to be born and raised in the house where their father was born. I was. On an old farm in northeastern Ohio—halfway between Canton and Alliance—of sixty acres; a barn, outbuildings, orchards, a pond, a nice-sized woods, and a back lane enclosed by an ancient rail fence. The fields hadn't been plowed in forty years. All was nicely wild and great for exploring.

My parents were teachers and great readers. So were their children . . . whether we wanted to be or not. As a child I was always puzzled by the lack of books in our neighbors' houses. Our house was overrun with reading materials; the overflow filled half the attic.

I started to read at four and have never stopped. As a child I read books indiscriminately—juvenile or adult, junk or classic. Now, as a writer, remembering my own reading habits as a child, I know I can't possibly imagine another child's interests or reading level and try to satisfy them, but only hope that what pleases and interests me has the same appeal for other readers.

While attending a local college I decided I wanted to be a nurse (one goes through stages) and went off to California to the Los Angeles County School of Nursing. Seeing what a nurse actually did for a living was a great education. I quit after one semester, got a job, and went to Los Angeles City College at night. California was then, as now, a great place in which to be young, but two years there was enough. A friend and I moved to New York City with $250 between us and a lot of optimism.

Writing books of my own was never one of my dreams. (What I dreamed of being at fourteen was a Cadillac owner; at seventeen I wanted to be an archaeologist.) At thirty-two it occurred to me that it might be nice to write. I quit my job and took four years off to teach myself the craft. It was a long four years, full of hope, self-doubt, and anxiety. The first short story sold, and the second, and then nothing until the four years were almost up, and *Children of Morrow* was bought by Four Winds Press. With a great sense of relief I went out and got myself a job. And got to work on *The Lion's Cub*.

Since then I've averaged about a book a year. I'm working on number fourteen now and am still unsure about how to write. One slowly learns what *not* to do, but is never sure of the other. I work slowly but routinely; if I waited for inspiration I'd never finish a chapter. Writing at book length is a matter of discipline, of sitting down at the desk each day, every day, whether I want to or not. Some days writing is fun; some days it isn't.

Every time there is any danger of getting pleased with myself, all that is necessary to bring me back to reality is a trip to any library. There on the shelves are the hundreds and hundreds of books that have lived for fifty years or a hundred, books so well-written, so universally human, that they speak to each new generation of readers, and they teach me what to aim for, if not how to get there.

Bibliography

1973	*Children of Morrow*
1974	*The Lion's Cub*
1976	*Treasures of Morrow*
1977	*The Delikon*
1977	*The Rains of Eridan*
1979	*The Lost Star*
1980	*Return to Earth*
1980	*This Time of Darkness*
1981	*Another Heaven, Another Earth*
1982	*The Bell Tree*
1984	*The Shepherd Moon*
1987	*ORVIS*
1988	*The Dawn Palace*
1989	*Away Is a Strange Place to Be*

Lee Bennett Hopkins

PHOTO: JEFFREY WEIN

I was born on April 13, 1938, in Scranton, Pennsylvania. My parents moved to Newark, New Jersey, where I grew up and lived until I graduated from Kean College (formerly Newark State Teachers College).

My parents separated when I was twelve, leaving my mother to support me, a younger brother, and a sister. Although life was very hard at times, I enjoyed a wonderful, carefree, independent teenage life. Those early years became the plots of my first three novels, *Mama, Wonder Wheels,* and *Mama and Her Boys.* Many of the episodes in these books stemmed directly from true experiences.

I knew from the age of thirteen that I wanted to be a classroom teacher. I reached that goal in 1960, and taught for six years in an elementary school in Fair Lawn, New Jersey.

Leaving Fair Lawn, I went to New York City to take a position at Bank Street College of Education, where I had received my master's degree. It was there, working with educators and children in Harlem, that I began to write. My early works were journal articles, followed by professional books, and finally books for children and young adults.

My career began to soar when my first anthology, *Don't You Turn Back: Poems by Langston Hughes,* received an American Library Notable Book Award. Since that time I have done over seventy volumes focusing on a wide variety of subjects.

Having found that poetry can truly turn youngsters around, and that so little poetry was well-used throughout the grades, I saw that a great charge of mine was to bring the genre to children in different ways.

Several of my collections deal with the work of an individual poet. In addition to Langston Hughes, I have done *Crickets and*

*Bullfrogs and Whispers of Thunder: Poems and Pictures by Harry Behn,
Rainbows are Made: Poems by Carl Sandburg,* and *Voyages: Poems by
Walt Whitman.* My objective in doing such collections is to present
readers with a body of these great American writers in a pleasant,
unthreatening way.

Since my writing life, like my personal life, is eclectic, I never
know what book project will appear next. On a typical day I might
be juggling several projects for several different age levels—working
on an "I Can Read" book, compiling a young adult anthology, and
creating books or articles for adult readers.

Fortunately, for me, the writing bug stung and the wound
never healed. I hope it never, ever does!

Bibliography

Books for Young Adults

1979	*Mama*
1979	*Wonder Wheels*
1981	*Mama and Her Boys*

Edited Poetry Collections

1969	*Don't Turn Back: Poems by Langston Hughes,* illus. by Ann Grifalconi
1970	*Me! A Book of Poems,* illus. by Talavaldis Stubis
1971	*Zoo! A Book of Poems,* illus. by Robert Frankenberg
1972	*Girls Can, Too! A Book of Poems,* illus. by Emily McCully
1974	*I Really Want to Feel Good about Myself: Poems by Former Drug Addicts* (with Sunna Rasch)
1974	*Poetry on Wheels,* illus. by Frank Aloise
1976	*Potato Chips and a Slice of Moon: Poems You'll Like* (with M. Arenstein), illus. by Wayne Blickenstaff
1977	*Monsters, Ghoulies, and Creepy Creatures: Fantastic Stories and Poems,* illus. by V. Rosenberry
1980	*Elves, Fairies, and Gnomes,* illus. by R. Hoffman
1982	*Circus! Circus!,* illus. by John O'Brien
1982	*Rainbows Are Made: Poems by Carl Sandburg,* illus. by Fritz Eichenberg
1983	*A Song in Stone: City Poems,* illus. by Anna Held Audette
1984	*Surprises: An "I Can Read" Book of Poems,* illus. by Meagan Lloyd
1985	*Munching: Poems about Eating,* illus. by Nelle Davis
1986	*The Sea Is Calling Me,* illus. by Walter Gaffney-Kessel

1987	*Click, Rumble, Roar: Poems about Machines,* illus. by Anna Held Audette
1987	*Dinosaurs,* illus. by Murray Tinkleman
1988	*Side By Side: Poems to Read Together,* illus. by Hilary Knight
1988	*Voyages: Poems by Walt Whitman,* illus. by Charles Mikolaycak

Books for Younger Readers

1976	*I Loved Rose Ann,* illus. by Ingrid Fetz
1983	*How Do You Make an Elephant Float? and Other Delicious Riddles,* illus. by Rosekrans Hoffman

Books of Poetry

1970	*This Street's for Me!,* illus. by Ann Grifalconi
1972	*Charlie's World: A Book of Poems,* illus. by Charles Robinson
1974	*Kim's Place and Other Poems,* illus. by Lawrence DiFiori

Books for Adults—Nonfiction (selected)

1969	*Books Are by People: Interviews with 104 Authors and Illustrators of Books for Young Children*
1969	*Creative Activities for the Gifted Child*
1972	*Pass the Poetry, Please!*
1975	*Do You Know What Day Tomorrow Is? A Teacher's Almanac* (with M. Arenstein)
1980	*The Best of Book Bonanza*

Hadley Irwin

PHOTO: SHIRLEY WALROD

Whenever Hadley Irwin is asked to make a public appearance, she always insists upon having a comfortable chair on stage where she can sit down and rest, for the author is the product of over 124 years of living, as well as more than 75 years of teaching on every educational level from kindergarten to graduate school. As one startled teenage reader exclaimed at a recent autographing session, "Hadley Irwin is two!"

Hadley Irwin, however, maintains that numbers lie, and she insists that when it comes to writing for young adults, $1 + 1 = 1$. Something happened with the publication of *The Lilith Summer* in 1979 when Lee Hadley and Ann Irwin were professors of English at Iowa State University. The pen name Hadley Irwin suddenly became a real, living entity and an author who, we quickly discovered, was a better writer than either Lee Hadley or Ann Irwin alone. We also discovered that collaboration was fun, that teenage readers were an intelligent and discriminating audience, and that writing for this age group was a definite challenge.

Sources of ideas for our books have ranged from a photo in a newspaper and a footnote in a history book to an overheard conversation in a school hallway. The Hadley/Irwin team had just finished speaking to a gymnasium full of junior high students and the two of us were dodging our way down the hall with locker doors slamming on all sides when we noticed two girls engaged in a rather heated argument. One girl stood defiantly with hands on her hips, eyed the other girl, and said, "He's *not* my boyfriend! He's just a friend who happens to be a boy!" We knew that instant what the next book would be. It was *Moon and Me*.

Some of our books deal with more serious concerns: *Abby, My Love*, with incest; *So Long at the Fair*, with suicide. Though such subjects are difficult, we attempt to treat them with honesty and lack of sensationalism. We have also written books which deal with the concerns of Native Americans, African-Americans, and Japanese-Americans, and in doing so have gained a greater understanding of the beauty of ethnicity, which we hope we have shared with our readers.

If there is one idea or theme or hope that Hadley Irwin wishes to convey to her readers it is that no matter how tragic an event may be, there is always humor alive somewhere in the world, that the human spirit can and does triumph, and that with help and love and understanding most problems of the teen years can be lived through. She knows, because she has lived through the teen years twice—once as Lee Hadley and once as Ann Irwin.

At the present time, Lee Hadley teaches creative writing at Iowa State University. Ann Irwin is retired from teaching and, as professor emeritus, resides with her husband on a small Iowa lake.

Bibliography

1979   *The Lilith Summer*
1980   *We Are Mesquakie, We Are One*
1981   *Bring to a Boil and Separate*
1981   *Moon and Me*
1982   *What about Grandma?*
1984   *I Be Somebody*
1985   *Abby, My Love*
1987   *Kim/Kimi*
1988   *So Long at the Fair*
1988   *Writing Young Adult Novels* (with Jeannette Eyerly)

M. E. Kerr

An entry in my baby book written by my mother when I was twelve complains, *Marijane isn't interested in anything! Stays up in her room after school and nights after dinner, writing stories! Goes to dancing class by force, but gave up piano! Tried knitting. Didn't like that, either!*

I wanted to be a writer all my life.

In the small town of Auburn, New York, where I grew up, there was a famous writer named Samuel Hopkins Adams. I would pedal past his house on my bike just to see where a real author lived.

Without my mother knowing it, she was one of the reasons I wanted to tell stories so badly. There was no greater gossip in all of Cayuga County, perhaps in all of New York State, maybe in all the world. I wasn't *always* up in my room. Often I was right around the corner of the living room listening to her begin every phone conversation with "Wait till you hear this! . . ." Certainly I was at the dining room table during lunch and dinner when my mother turned our small town into a wonderland of intrigue, skullduggery, and mystery. She knew everything that was going on, and if she didn't her girlfriends and her hairdresser did.

My father, a mayonnaise manufacturer, pretended to be above such scandalous talk, reminding her that he did business in that town and she should hold her tongue, but he listened as spellbound as my brothers and I did. She had a way about her when it came to describing what the neighbors were up to. We called her Ida, the Town Crier.

My father was the other reason I wanted to write. He read aloud to me from the time I was a baby. When he wasn't reading to me, he was sitting in his big armchair with his eyeshield on, smoking a pipe and reading—everything! Newspapers and magazines, nonfiction, fiction, classics, and the Book-of-the-Month. He was deaf in one ear and wore a hearing aid (not perfected in those days), so he was an introverted man with few friends, awkward in social situations. He did things by himself when we kids weren't available. He rowed and sailed and skated and *read*.

From my parents, I learned all the small-town values, prejudices, and traditions. Until I went away to boarding school during World War II, I thought every family was like mine, and all towns like Auburn.

Most of my YA books have chronicled the lessons I learned after leaving home, when I finally had other lives to contrast to and compare with mine . . . and when I gained the distance necessary to see who I really was or wasn't.

I like to write about the outsider because, when I got away, I knew I'd always been away and I'd never really go back, except in fiction.

The stories that compel me are about differences in people: understanding them, and understanding those who can't accept them . . ., surviving, with humor, others' and your own slings and arrows . . ., trying to make some sense of it all, never losing sight of the power love lends.

Bibliography

1972   *Dinky Hocker Shoots Smack*
1973   *If I Love You, Am I Trapped Forever?*
1974   *The Son of Someone Famous*
1975   *Is That You, Miss Blue?*
1975   *Love Is a Missing Person*
1977   *I'll Love You When You're More Like Me*
1978   *Gentlehands*
1981   *Little Little*
1982   *What I Really Think of You*
1983   *Me Me Me Me Me*
1984   *Him She Loves?*
1985   *I Stay Near You*
1986   *Night Kites*
1987   *Fell*
1989   *Fell Back*

Norma Klein

I grew up in New York City, where I still live with my husband, Erwin Fleissner, who recently became dean of sciences and mathematics at Hunter College. My younger brother, Victor, and I attended private schools—Dalton until high school, Elisabeth Irwin for ninth to twelfth grades. My father, who died in 1977, was a Freudian psychoanalyst; my mother graduated college at the age of seventy-eight.

I've always loved New York, which is the background for many of my novels. It seemed to me when I began writing books for kids that most teenage novels were set in the Midwest or the suburbs. I wanted to portray the kind of teenager I was and the kind my kids were—bright, thoughtful, idealistic people, not cheerleaders or football stars. I've tried to write the kinds of books I would have liked to read while in high school or college, books with the complexity of novels for adults but with a teenage protagonist.

I started my college years at Cornell and transferred after one year to Barnard, from which I graduated in 1960. For the next three years I was in graduate school in Slavic languages at Columbia, thinking I would become a college professor. But my main love had always been writing, and when I got married in 1963 at the age of twenty-five, I decided to devote myself full-time to that.

My first published work was a short story, "Ceremony of Innocence," which was published when I was nineteen in a small literary magazine, *The Grecourt Review*. For the next decade I published about sixty short stories for adults, several of which were anthologized in *The Best American Short Stories* or *Prize Stories: The O. Henry Awards*. My children were born in 1967 (Jen) and 1970 (Katie). At first I wanted to write and illustrate my own picture books since I had always been seriously interested in art. Although that didn't work out, I did begin writing novels for older kids. The first one, *Mom, the Wolf Man and Me,* appeared in 1972.

For the next two decades I alternated writing novels for teenagers with novels for adults. I enjoy going back and forth between the two because there is still much less censorship in the field of adult fiction and I like writing some of the time from the point of view of adults as well as trying multiple viewpoints, longer length, and other more experimental techniques.

I'm an ardent feminist and hope that is, in a subtle way, reflected in my fiction. One of my favorite hobbies is reading. I prefer realistic books about contemporary life told with directness and humor. My favorite writers are Jane Austen and Anton Chekhov.

I get my ideas from everyday life, from stories told to me by my friends and children, and from daydreaming while waiting for the bus. I've always enjoyed the act of writing and hope to continue for the rest of my life. I'm a morning person who, while working on a novel, types ten pages every day. I don't yet have a word processor but am considering getting one.

Bibliography

Books for Young Adults

1973	*It's Not What You Expect*
1974	*Taking Sides*
1976	*Hiding*
1977	*It's Okay If You Don't Love Me*
1978	*Love Is One of the Choices*
1980	*Breaking Up*
1982	*The Queen of the What Ifs*
1983	*Beginner's Love*
1983	*Bizou*
1984	*Angel Face*
1984	*Snapshots*
1985	*Give and Take*
1985	*The Cheerleader*
1985	*Family Secrets*
1986	*Going Backwards*
1987	*Older Men*
1987	*My Life as a Body*

1988	*Now That I Know*
1988	*No More Saturday Nights*
1989	*Learning How to Fall*

Books for Younger Readers

1972	*Mom, the Wolf Man and Me*
1973	*Confessions of an Only Child*
1975	*What It's All About*
1978	*Tomboy*
1980	*A Honey of a Champ*
1981	*Robbie and the Leap Year Blues*
1983	*Baryshnikov's Nutcracker*

Picture Books

1973	*Girls Can Be Anything*
1974	*Naomi in the Middle*
1974	*If I Had My Way*
1974	*Dinosaur's Housewarming Party*
1974	*A Train for Jane*
1975	*Blue Trees, Red Sky*
1979	*Visiting Pamela*

Books for Adults

1972	*Love and Other Euphemisms* (short stories)
1973	*Give Me One Good Reason*
1974	*Coming to Life*
1976	*Girls Turn Wives*
1981	*Domestic Arrangements*
1982	*Wives and Other Women*
1983	*The Swap*
1983	*Sextet in A Minor* (short stories)
1984	*Lovers*
1987	*American Dreams*
1989	*The World as It Is*

Novelizations

1975	*Sunshine*
1975	*The Sunshine Years*
1977	*Sunshine Christmas*
1979	*French Postcards*

Gordon Korman

I was born in Montreal, Canada, on October 23, 1963. When I was seven, my family moved to Toronto. It was there that my writing career began, almost by accident. My seventh-grade English teacher (who was actually a phys. ed. teacher relegated to English class due to staff cutbacks) told us we were to spend the remaining four months of school writing novels. So I did. *This Can't Be Happening at Macdonald Hall* was ultimately published in January of 1978. It turned out to be a launchpad for four more books about the characters Bruno and Boots, including my latest novel, *The Zucchini Warriors*, and has been translated into French, Swedish, Norwegian, and Canton Chinese. In spite of all this, I still got a B+ in English that term. Then and now, neatness counts.

Even after *This Can't Be Happening at Macdonald Hall* was published, and was followed by a couple of sequels, I never took writing seriously as a career. Then, in eleventh grade, we filled out those career-interest computer questionnaires designed to keep the market for No. 2 pencils vibrant. According to the computer, I had what it took to be an electrical engineer. I was blown away, and it took a minute to figure out why. I had three books out and two more awaiting publication. I had to become a writer fast before I wound up in engineering school.

I went to NYU in New York City to study film and television production, but switched to dramatic writing when I realized I had no aptitude for holding the camera steady. Adjusting to New York City became the subject of *Don't Care High*, although the high school in the story is really my alma mater in Toronto—a school so apathetic and blasé that the closest thing to school spirit I can remember in the four years I spent there was the semester my homeroom led the school in overdue library books. *Son of Interflux* and *A Semester in the Life of a Garbage Bag* also take place in the New York area.

My books are humorous and are intended primarily to entertain. Lately, it seems as though the older a kid gets, the less fun stuff there is to read. I want my writing to be the exception to that unfortunate rule. I devoutly hope there will be a lot more. We lose so many readers between sixth grade and tenth grade.

I keep the stories enjoyable for my readers by keeping them enjoyable for me. Confession: I know it's impolite to laugh at my own jokes, but I really crack myself up while I'm writing.

Bibliography

Books for Young Adults

1985	*Don't Care High*
1986	*Son of Interflux*
1987	*A Semester in the Life of a Garbage Bag*

Books for Middle Grade/Junior High Readers

1980	*I Want to Go Home*
1981	*Who Is Bugs Potter?*
1982	*Our Man Weston*
1983	*Bugs Potter: Live at Mickaninny*
1984	*No Coins, Please*
1989	*Radio Fifth Grade*

Bruno and Boots Series

1978	*This Can't Be Happening at Macdonald Hall*
1979	*Go Jump in the Pool*
1980	*Beware the Fish*
1983	*The War with Mr. Wizzle*
1988	*The Zucchini Warriors*

Kathryn Lasky

I n the late 1950s when I was growing up, the world, except for the place where I was, seemed rather exciting. Sputnik had just been launched, Jerry Lee Lewis married his thirteen-year-old cousin, and Errol Flynn died in the arms of his fifteen-year-old girlfriend. I was a freshman in an all-girls high school declining Latin nouns and struggling with quadratic equations. My life seemed very dull in comparison. In my secret life, however, I entertained the notion of another self that was not the teeny, tiny teen wife of a rock-and-roll singer or the mistress of an aging debauched matinee idol, but a writer. I had been seduced hopelessly by that art, first as a reader and then as a secret writer and spinner of tales that I showed to no one.

I still don't really know when I first began thinking of myself as a real writer. It might have been relatively recently—like when I first got paid for a manuscript. But that might have been only when I first dared to call myself a writer to the world at large. I think perhaps I always felt that this was my profession, announced or unannounced, proclaimed or unproclaimed, paid or unpaid. I have always been a writer. But if forced to say precisely when the idea really took root I think it was when I was very young. I can remember one summer night in northern Indiana, where we had a lakeside cottage, when we were returning from the A&W root beer stand in an old two-tone blue Chevy convertible. My dad was driving, and the top was down. I was in the back with my sister Martha and I had my head flung back against the back of the seat. I was looking up at the sky hoping to find the Big Dipper. But there were no stars at all that night. The clouds, however, thick and wooly, were rolling in, and suddenly an image struck me. "It's a sheepback sky," I said into the soft air whizzing by. My mom heard

114

me and turned around. "Kathy," she said, "you should be a writer." That, I suppose, was when the notion first took seed.

I've written books for very young children as well as books for teenagers. Occasionally I even lapse into nonfiction. Several of my books are joint ventures with my husband, Chris, who is a professional photographer and filmmaker. Those include *Tall Ships, Dollmaker, The Weaver's Gift, Sugaring Time,* and *A Baby for Max* (which our son wrote about his experience of becoming a brother). But even in my nonfiction books, telling a story is more important than reciting the facts. Real stories can be either fiction or nonfiction.

Bibliography

Books for Young Adults

1981	*The Night Journey*
1983	*Beyond the Divide*
1984	*Prank*
1985	*Home Free*
1986	*Pageant*
1988	*The Bone Wars*

Books for Younger Readers

1973	*Agatha's Alphabet*
1976	*I Have Four Names for My Grandfather*
1977	*Tugboats Never Sleep*
1978	*Tall Ships*
1979	*My Island Grandma*
1981	*The Weaver's Gift*
1982	*Dollmaker*
1982	*Jem's Island*
1983	*Sugaring Time*
1984	*A Baby for Max*
1985	*Puppeteer*
1988	*Sea Swan*

Other Books (written by Kathryn Lasky Knight)

1984	*Atlantic Circle*
1986	*Trace Elements*
1989	*The Widow of Oz*

Madeleine L'Engle

I was born in New York City after the armistice which proclaimed the end of the war that was to end all wars. I have lived in a century of war, and it has made me ask many questions.

I was an unsuccessful, non-achieving schoolchild. Because I was slightly lame and not good at team sports, my teachers decided that I was not intelligent. I learned quickly that there was no point in doing homework for them; they were going to put it down, or hold it up for ridicule. So I would go home, dump down my books and not look at them, and then I wrote and read and dreamed. I built up a body of work which I would never have done had I been happy and successful at school. I wrote poems, plays, stories, and journals, and my unsympathetic teachers inadvertently pushed me into a discipline of writing that has stood me in good stead.

When I was in sixth grade I won a poetry prize, and my homeroom teacher said, "Madeleine couldn't possibly have written that poem. She must have copied it from somewhere. She's not very bright, you know." My mother went to the school, carrying the large quantity of work I had done instead of homework, and it had to be conceded that Madeleine had very likely written that poem after all. So I was set on my path as a writer very early.

When I was twelve we moved to the French Alps trying to find air clean enough for my father to breathe. He had been gassed in that First World War, and mustard gas just goes on eating away at the lungs. It took my father until I was nearly eighteen to finish coughing his lungs out. What were my parents to do with me? I was put in an English boarding school, where I was taught Anglican virtues (which I have been spending the rest of my life unlearning) but very little Anglican theology. And I kept on writing.

When I was fourteen we returned to the United States, and I spent four happy, productive years at Ashley Hall in Charleston, South Carolina, where my teachers at last saw potential in a shy, introverted girl, and encouraged me. Holidays were spent in a rambling old cottage on a beautiful stretch of Florida beach.

After graduating from Ashley Hall I went to Smith College when the English department was at its magnificent height. I majored in English literature, had superb professors, women who today would be called "role models," who were so on fire with enthusiasm for their subjects that we students couldn't help catching their flame. I continued to write, to work in the theatre, both acting and helping my own plays to be produced. I graduated with honors and moved to New York City and to a Greenwich Village apartment with an assortment of friends. I worked in the theatre as an actress, though I was always general understudy or assistant stage manager, with maybe a few walk-on bits and a couple of lines. But I worked, and I wrote my first two published novels, and met actor Hugh Franklin in *The Cherry Orchard* and married him in *The Joyous Season*. We had a baby and moved to northwestern Connecticut to continue our family away from the tensions and strains of the city. We ran a general store in a small dairy farm village where there were more cows than people, and were deeply involved in the life of the village. After nine years we returned to New York with three children, and Hugh continued his work in the theatre.

I continued to write but, after my first five successful books, accumulated a vast number of rejection slips. *A Wrinkle in Time* was rejected by every major publisher as being too strange a book and much too difficult for children. In 1962 Farrar, Straus & Giroux risked publishing it, and in 1963 it won the Newbery medal.

I have written about my life and my struggles as a writer and a woman in several nonfiction books, the most recent and most directly autobiographical being *Two Part Invention*, published in 1989 by FSG.

Our children continued to grow, went to college, left the nest. I continued to write and Hugh to act, and to enjoy each other and life; once we could afford to we divided our time between Manhattan Island and northwestern Connecticut in the Litchfield Hills. During the last two years of our forty-year marriage, Hugh and I travelled widely for the U.S. Information Agency, doing dramatic readings from my books and going to such diverse places as Egypt, Austria, and Hong Kong.

After Hugh's death in the autumn of 1986, I continued to write, travel, and lecture extensively. Thus far I have written approximately thirty-nine books (I am not good with numbers, am considerably better with words). I have the joy of living with my granddaughters, who are both in college in New York. Frequently I cook for twenty or more people, but the bargain is that I do the cooking and not the washing up.

And I continue to write and write and write.

Bibliography

Books for Young Adults

1949	*And Both Were Young*
1960	*Meet the Austins*
1962	*A Wrinkle in Time*
1963	*The Moon by Night*
1965	*Camilla*
1965	*The Arm of the Starfish*
1968	*The Young Unicorns*
1969	*Dance in the Desert*
1973	*A Wind in the Door*
1974	*Prayers for Sunday*
1974	*Everyday Prayers*
1976	*Dragons in the Waters*
1978	*A Swiftly Tilting Planet*
1980	*The Anti-Muffins*
1980	*A Ring of Endless Light*
1982	*The Sphinx at Dawn*
1984	*A House Like a Lotus*
1986	*Many Waters*

Other Books

1945	*The Small Pain*
1946	*Ilsa*
1957	*A Winter's Love*
1964	*The Twenty-four Days before Christmas*
1966	*The Love Letters*
1967	*The Journey with Jonah*
1969	*Lines Scribbled on an Envelope and Other Poems*
1971	*A Circle of Quiet*

Myron Levoy

I was born and grew up in New York City. Times were hard and toys were few, but I remember from a very early age constant trips to the library with my mother and brother, and the smell and feel of books. I recall writing a story of my own when I was eight about a flower growing out of a crack in the pavement. Would the flower survive? Would it be crushed underfoot? I can't remember how it ended, but I know I loved writing it.

When I was nine or ten I imagined being, in turn, an aviator, a baseball player (centerfield), a detective, and a cowboy. As I walked to and from school, or rode the subways, or lay in bed late on Sunday mornings, stories whirled in my head. Sometimes I wrote a few paragraphs or a chapter until a new heroic adventure, far more magnificent, blew the present story away.

In junior high we did choral speaking, a popular activity in those days. Our class won third place in a citywide contest. Our teacher thought we should have been first, but we had been scared out of our wits on the gigantic stage of the Brooklyn Academy of Music. But never mind—Eileen P. Delaney, our teacher, mentor, and friend had shown us something that has remained with me all my life: words alone, without music, can sing.

So I started writing poetry and, in high school, I edited the poetry column in our school newspaper, the *Newton X-Ray*. This wasn't exactly the usual thing for a pre-engineering, technical-course student. But I had that other side to me, as they say. I'd always done well in math and the sciences, and I truly liked chemistry and physics. In short, I went to City College of New York and to Purdue University for degrees in chemical engineering. But writing, nevertheless, remained my first love.

And the would-be writer grew up, became an engineer, married, moved to Connecticut and then to New Jersey, had two children, and did engineering by day and wrote by night. Wrote poetry and short stories which appeared in the quarterly magazines, wrote plays which were performed in New York experimental theatres, and one day wrote a short story for his children, Debbie and David. The story evolved into a book of seven short stories, *The Witch of Fourth Street*, and a new direction, writing for children and young adults, began.

A few words about my work: my young adult books are often about the loners, the "outsiders" who must make a choice. Will they be true to their inner selves, or will they follow the crowd? For example, there's Alan in *Alan and Naomi*, who befriends a "crazy" girl though he believes he'll be ridiculed and shunned by his friends; and there's Ramon, a ghetto boy in *A Shadow Like a Leopard*, torn between two worlds, who carries a knife but writes poetry. Their choices are painful, tentative, and, in some instances, courageous. They must grow, like that flower in the pavement, alone, unique, and not be crushed. And so the theme recurs, like an arc, from the eight-year-old to me, here, now.

Bibliography

Books for Young Adults

1977	*Alan and Naomi*
1981	*A Shadow Like a Leopard*
1984	*Three Friends*
1986	*Pictures of Adam*

Books for Younger Readers

1972	*Penny Tunes and Princesses*
1972	*The Witch of Fourth Street*
1984	*The Hanukkah of Great-Uncle Otto*
1988	*The Magic Hat of Mortimer Wintergreen*

Robert Lipsyte

I became a YA novelist one night in 1965 in Las Vegas. I was there to cover the heavyweight championship match between Muhammad Ali and Floyd Patterson for *The New York Times*, and I took an old manager out to dinner to pump him for information, to get answers to questions, which is what reporters do. But he left me with questions instead of answers. He told me about a gym he once owned in a Manhattan slum, and how he would sit at the top of the three dark, narrow twisting flights of stairs that led to his gym, waiting for a kid so tough and motivated and desperate that he would come up those stairs alone, at night, and running scared. Such a kid, he said, would have a shot at becoming somebody, a "contender."

All the rest of the night, and through the prizefight and back to New York, I wondered what kind of kid would come up those dark and twisting stairs, what would be happening in his life to set him on that risky path, and what would happen once he reached the top. There was no one to interview for that story. Only my imagination could answer those questions. So I started to write about a black teenager named Alfred Brooks whose life in Harlem was so dead-ended and dangerous that he dared to challenge himself to break out and create a new life. The story became *The Contender*, and when Harper and Row published it in 1967 I felt as though I was on my way to becoming a contender, too.

I always wanted to be a novelist. I was born and raised in apartments in New York City, but I spent my summers in upstate New York, where my parents, who were schoolteachers, had built a house. I was very fat as a kid, and I hated the summertime because you couldn't hide yourself inside layers of clothing. I hid out, reading and writing and daydreaming. It was a perfect childhood for a writer. When I was fourteen I lied about my age and got a job mowing the gigantic lawn of a perfectionist. I lost a great deal of weight that summer, exactly how much I never knew, because I had never wanted to know exactly how much I weighed in the first place. Whenever the number 200 started to roll up on the scale, I bailed out.

At nineteen, after graduation from Columbia, I became a copy boy in the sports department of *The New York Times*. It was to be a summer job before I went west to seek my fortune writing novels and screenplays. But I fell in love with the thunderous roar of the presses (they actually roared in those days), and I spent fourteen years at the *Times* before I quit to write novels and screenplays. During the next eleven years, I also wrote four more YA novels, three of them about Bobby Marks, a daydreamer who loses a great deal of weight, exactly how much he would never be sure.

In 1982, I became the sports essayist for the CBS News broadcast "Sunday Morning with Charles Kuralt." It was to be a summer job to get me out of the house before I started a new YA novel. But I fell in love with television, the joy of collaborating with others, the magic of making little movies, the access to people's lives and thoughts, and, yes, the image of myself on the screen. After four years at CBS, I moved on to NBC News as a network correspondent specializing in sports.

Television is fun—a friend of mine calls it a perpetual seventh-grade class trip—but nothing is as much fun as creating a world on a piece of paper, especially for readers whose minds are still open to change and possibility, who still dare to climb three flights of dark, narrow, twisting stairs, alone at night and running scared.

Bibliography

Books for Young Adults

1967	*The Contender*
1970	*Assignment Sports*
1977	*One Fat Summer*
1978	*Free to Be Muhammad Ali*
1981	*Summer Rules*
1982	*Jock and Jill*
1982	*The Summerboy*

1984   *Assignment Sports* (revised)

Other Books

1964   *Nigger* (the autobiography of Dick Gregory)
1966   *The Masculine Mystique*
1972   *Something Going* (with Steve Cady)
1974   *Liberty Two*
1975   *Sportsworld: An American Dreamland*

Katie Letcher Lyle

I always thought of myself as a writer, which I suppose was useful in becoming one, and I was helped along by my friends and family, who found writing less troublesome than most of my other activities, which included acting (my family had to *go* to everything I was in), playing the ukulele very loudly, and trying out for every singing contest that came along, along with some disastrous efforts to become a horsewoman, as all my friends were (they were all lots more coordinated than I). I actually had a poem published in a kids' magazine when I was eight, so I learned early that what I wrote could appear in print.

My first novel was published twenty-five years afterwards when I was thirty-three, and to my great surprise the world found it to be something called a "young adult" novel. Received warmly into that field, which was very big in the seventies, I did four more YA novels, but always with the feeling that that was not really my field.

I've always taught in addition to writing—everything from Sunday school to college, but usually I've taught teenagers, so they provided my mind with people and subjects for novels.

Then in 1982 I was asked to write a book about train wreck songs, a popular American phenomenon from about 1890 until around 1930. I discovered research and fell in love. Other changes took place around then: I began to teach at Elderhostels and found I loved teaching the elderly as much as I loved teaching teens. As a result of the train wreck songbook, I began singing again after leaving the world in peace for twenty-five years. With two friends, I traveled throughout the South, presenting concerts of the songs in the book, and finding other research topics, which keep me busy to this day. Now I have retired from college teaching at Southern

Seminary Junior College to do workshops and teach Elderhostels in many subjects: creative writing, historical research, Virginia folklore, even foods and wines of the Old Dominion. I still hope to stun the world with the Great American Novel, female version. I have been writing short fiction recently, along with my historical research.

Writing is a wonderful life, but it is not the easy one some folks imagine it to be. I maintain a rigorous schedule of writing every day, and I don't allow writer's block to get in my way. When it does, I read books about how to write, or edit other things I've written. I try to remember that writing is a craft, not a mystery, and that, with practice, anyone with the bent for a thing can improve on the doing of that thing. I put my hope in that thought. If I waited for inspiration, I'd never finish anything. When I'm working, I don't answer the phone and I don't get up to defrost the refrigerator. Instead, I keep a notepad by the computer, on which I save those seductive messages that come to mind: The plants are dying! The clothes need washing! I forgot to call Gertrude! Once jotted down, they can be forgotten until I'm ready to deal with them. My husband, children, and friends respect my writing time, as I try to respect what is important to them.

So I work at writing, honing my craft all the time, not expecting miracles but hoping that inspiration is like happiness: it is said that if you seek it you'll never find it. But I tell you that if you will pursue the craft of writing seriously and with respect, eventually inspiration will find you.

Bibliography

Books for Young Adults

1973   *I Will Go Barefoot All Summer for You*
1974   *Fair Day, and Another Step Begun*
1976   *The Golden Shores of Heaven*
1981   *Dark But Full of Diamonds*
1982   *Finders Weepers*

Other Books

1964   *Lyrics of Three Women* (poems with Maude Rubin and May Miller)
1984   *Scalded to Death by the Steam* (historical nonfiction)
1986   *The Man Who Wanted Seven Wives* (historical nonfiction)

Television Scripts

1977–82 "Footsteps" (four programs on parenting)

Anne McCaffrey

My eyes are green, my hair is silver and I freckle: the rest is subject to change without notice.

Getting born on an unusual day made a good start to becoming a science-fiction writer: April 1st was Holy Thursday that Year of the Fire Tiger. April 1926 also happened to be the month in which Hugo Gernsbach published the first dedicated science-fiction magazines—*Amazing Stories* and *Fantastic Stories*.

Having highly individualistic parents was another rung up: my father was an infantry colonel and Ph.D. who became a military governor in WWII, and my mother was a very good real estate saleswoman. They both read, and read to their children. The colonel read a mean Kipling! My mother went in for mysteries and introduced me to A. Merritt.

Being a totally uncompromising egregious domineering opinionated brat was also significant because *no one* would play with me, so I learned to amuse myself at a very early age. The household cat, Thomas, became my playmate and confidant. I got smitten at nine by Horse, which is probably how I so easily arrived at the Dragons of Pern as "critters" to write about. If you were a lonely kid, wouldn't *you* like a forty-foot fire-breathing telepathic teleporting dragon as *your* best friend?

In point of fact the three Harper Hall books—*Dragonsong, Dragonsinger,* and *Dragondrums*—were written at the request of Jean Karl of Atheneum Press, who thought that perhaps more girls would become interested in science fiction if there were some young-adult female protagonists. She suggested I use another part of the planet Pern, which had already generated two books, *Dragonflight* and *Dragonquest*. It seemed an eminently sensible suggestion.

Some characters take off with a book despite an author's intentions. Menolly did this, being a composite of two young riders I know here in Ireland. Piemur, the hero of *Dragondrums*, sort of elbowed his way into *Dragonsinger*, imperiously demanding to help Menolly feed her fire-lizards.

Although I always knew I would be a writer, I didn't get started until my first son was born. I stole hours while Alec, and later Todd and Georgeanne, napped; winkled plot changes through my head as I did all the mechanical things a mother and housewife must get done; and used the money earned from magazine sales to hire a babysitter for a precious three hours a day in the summertime. Only after my daughter was going to school full-time did I finally have the un-mommied time to try novels.

I was lucky. No one ever mentioned to me that science fiction had a predominantly male readership. No one told me women weren't supposed to write science fiction. I entered the field in the mid-sixties when readers started looking for more viable plots and better characterization, when "Star Trek" had broadened the readership base.

Having spent most of my life on the East Coast, I moved to Ireland in 1970 with my mother and two younger children. Since then I've traveled all over the United States, Europe, and Australasia, lecturing and attending s-f conventions. I prefer to live in Ireland. These days I also own a farm and a private livery stable. We breed 3-Day Event and showjumping horses. The gal who manages it all for me and is our competition rider was one of the Menolly models!

When I'm asked *how* to write, I answer—"Tell me a story!"

Bibliography

Books for Young Adults

1969	*Decision at Doona*
1976	*Dragonsong*
1977	*Dragonsinger*
1977	*Get Off the Unicorn*
1978	*Dinosaur Planet*
1979	*Dragondrums*
1984	*Dinosaur Planet Survivors*
1986	*The Girl Who Heard Dragons*

Science Fiction

Non–Science Fiction

Robin McKinley

My mother says she used to prop me in a corner of the sofa before I was old enough to sit up by myself, and read aloud. There were always lots of books in the house; my father came back from his long overseas trips with his suitcases full of books and rolls of film. Wherever we moved— California, Japan, New England—my mother borrowed books by the shelf from the local (English-speaking) library, working tirelessly through the fiction racks from A to Z. When I got a little older I read her books too. As we moved so often and thus had often to start in on a new library, my mother sometimes brought the same title home twice. "Have I read this before?" she'd say, handing me a book across the breakfast table.

My father was in the navy, and I was an only child; and my parents were very strict about friends and after-school activities. I early found the world of books much more satisfactory than the unstable so-called real world. I can't remember the first time I read Frances Hodgson Burnett's *A Little Princess*; but this particular story, about a little girl all alone in a strange land who told stories so wonderful that she believed them herself, fascinated me. I never quite lived up to Sara Crewe's standard, but I tried awfully hard.

Writing has always been the other side of reading for me; it never occurred to me not to make up stories. Once I got old enough to realize that authorship existed as a thing one might aspire to, I knew it was for me. I even majored in English literature in college, a good indication of my fine bold disdain for anything so trivial as earning a living: I was going to be a writer, like Dickens and Hardy and Conrad. And Kipling and H. Rider Haggard and J.R.R. Tolkien. I still spend more of my time outside reality than in it; some of my favorite nonbook assists to Otherwhere are grand opera and long walks, the Oriental wings of museums, and John Huston's movie of *The Man Who Would Be King*. About the only irresistible attraction reality has ever exerted on me is in the shape of horses and riding. I don't pretend to explain this; there are few things more real than mucking out stalls or falling off on your head when you've forgotten to wear your hard hat.

As I began, so I go on. I still read compulsively, and I still travel a lot, although my life is now complicated by the possession

of several thousand books and a baby grand piano. I recently
bought a little house in a village about two-thirds of the way up the
Maine coast (much to my astonishment, as I had not considered
becoming a property owner), where books, piano, and accumulated
gear can settle with a sigh, and I can wander off as fancy takes me.
But I also have a part-time apartment in Manhattan, and I shuttle
cheerfully between the two when I'm not flying to Seattle or London
or plotting to get to Australia or back to the Far East. And
while my lilac-covered cottage is the light of my life, I still want a
castle in Scotland.

Bibliography

Books for Young Adults

1978   *Beauty: A Retelling of the Story of Beauty and the Beast*
1981   *The Door in the Hedge* (short stories)
1982   *The Blue Sword*
1984   *The Hero and the Crown*
1988   *Outlaws of Sherwood*

Other Books

1985   *Imaginary Lands* (editor—short stories)
1985   *Jungle Book Tales* (adapter)
1987   *Black Beauty* by Anna Sewell, illus. by Susan Jeffers (adapter)

Kevin Major

My father often referred to me as "the only Canadian in the family." I am the youngest of seven children and indeed the only one born after Newfoundland became a province of Canada in 1949. Prior to that, Newfoundland was a separate country. It is still separate from the rest of North America in lots of ways. It is an island, with a distinctive culture reflected in the way of life and speech of its people, as well as in its music and literature.

My part in that literature has been to tell stories of young people trying to balance the traditional values of their parents and grandparents with the values of life in the modern Newfoundland, where young people are just as much in tune with the popular culture of rock music, movies, and TV as young people anywhere.

Most of my novels are set in rural Newfoundland, communities which started centuries ago when people from England and Ireland came across the Atlantic to fish along our shores. My parents came from such a community, although I grew up in a part of the island very different from that experienced by most Newfoundlanders. I grew up in the town of Stephenville, which was adjacent to Ernest Harmon Air Force Base. During World War II the U.S. government set up two such bases in Newfoundland and my father came to Stephenville to work for the Americans. My own cultural influences therefore were varied—I fished for lobsters in the summertime with my father, I watched *Hockey Night in Canada* on TV, I toured B-52 bombers on the base, and I even studied French at school with a teacher from Morocco. It made for an interesting adolescence.

I finished high school and left Stephenville the same year that the Beatles released *Sergeant Pepper.* It was a wonderful time to be young and newly independent. Although I had a strong interest in writing, I headed for university to study pre-med. After three years and acceptance to medical school, I took a year away from studying. I travelled through parts of the West Indies and Europe for six months, and when I finally returned to university it was with plans to become a teacher and, hopefully, someday a published author.

I taught junior high and high school for four years—all in small coastal communities in Newfoundland. One of the things I noticed was that there were no characters in the books available for my students to read like the characters I saw in my classroom each day. Now that situation has changed.

Although I will always want to write about Newfoundland, I am at times drawn to setting my stories in other places, as I have done in *Dear Bruce Springsteen*. I am drawn as well to telling stories in different ways—as a multi-narrative, through letters, in "snapshots." I sometimes expect a lot of my readers, but through it all I hope they can feel the excitement that is fiction.

Bibliography

1978   *Hold Fast*
1980   *Far from Shore*
1984   *Thirty-Six Exposures*
1987   *Dear Bruce Springsteen*
1989   *Blood Red Ochre*

Sharon Bell Mathis

PHOTO: BILL TRAVIS

I was born in Atlantic City, New Jersey, and grew up in the Bedford-Stuyvesant section of Brooklyn, New York. I graduated from Holy Rosary Elementary School and St. Michael's Academy (a high school in Manhattan), where I enjoyed writing compositions in English classes—and winning singing contests.

My mother, Alice Frazier Bell, struggled to raise her four children alone, after my father (John W. Bell) decided that life was more exciting outside of his home.

Although my mother was a cardiac patient frequently admitted to hospitals, she managed to make a way out of no way for us. We lived in a lovely apartment and ate the best food she had to offer—generally rich stews and soups with plenty of homemade bread and puddings. Most of all, my mother was an avid reader and writer (a poem she wrote when she was seventeen was published in *The Negro History Bulletin*, and one of her short stories was published in *Ebony Jr.!*). Books were welcomed and enjoyed in my home. I grew up taking for granted that Black people could write, because my mother had bookcases filled with the works of Black writers.

I wrote my first poems and short stories perched on a fire escape high above the backyards and almost nestled in the trees. I was a preteen when I discovered that marvelous iron patio. It was my very own magic carpet. One of my earliest published stories for children was plainly called "The Fire Escape."

The books I write focus on children and teenagers simply because the characters constantly taking shape in my mind are never adults.

Writing allows me an opportunity to reenter childhood, to explore it anew, and to be enchanted.

Bibliography

Books for Young Adults

1970   *Brooklyn Story,* illus. by Charles Bible
1972   *Teacup Full of Roses*
1974   *Listen for the Fig Tree*
1977   *Cartwheels*

Books for Younger Readers

1971   *Sidewalk Story,* illus. by Leo Carty
1975   *The Hundred Penny Box,* illus. by Leo and Diane Dillon

Nonfiction

1973   *Ray Charles,* illus. by George Ford

Harry Mazer

I was born and grew up in New York City. My parents were Polish Jews, recent immigrants, workers, dressmakers. Four of us, including my little brother, lived in two rooms on the fourth floor of a brick house. Surrounding us were people like ourselves, young families, new to the country and filled with energy, ambition, and desire.

My school was P.S. 96 in the Bronx. After school I played in the streets, the empty lots, or the park nearby. I played marbles and chalked skipping games on the sidewalk. In gangs we played stick-ball, kick-the-can, Johnny-on-the-pony. Alone I climbed the rocks in the empty lots. In the mud near a leaky fire hydrant I scratched out rivers and lakes and built cities and palaces.

As a boy my plan was to read my way through the library, starting with the letter A. My father thought I was ruining my eyes. There were no writers in my family, no journalists, no actors, no entertainers. No teacher said, "Write: you have talent." In high school I wrote poetry and planned to be a chemist. After high school I joined the air force.

When I met Norma Fox I didn't know that she hungered to write. We fell in love, married. I was a veteran, a graduate of Union College in Schenectady, New York, with a liberal arts degree. I went to work as a bus driver. I wanted to change the world, not find myself. I worked on the railroad and in factories for ten years.

We began writing together. Learning to write. We had two children. We were to have four. We wrote at night and early in the morning. From the beginning, I wrote stories, showed them to Norma. We shared our ideas and fears; we disciplined, inspired, and supported one another.

137

Everything about my becoming a writer was strange. That I met Norma. That she, too, dreamed of writing. Strange that we both found pleasure and meaning in writing for the young. Strange that we both succeeded.

In each of my books there is invention and autobiography. Marcus Rosenbloom is very close to me. In *The Dollar Man* and *The War on Villa Street* I write about fathers and sons. In *Hey, Kid!* and *City Light* I write about beginnings, about how plans and certainties go astray. In *The Last Mission* and *When the Phone Rang* I write about surviving loss.

On one level all my stories, beginning with *Guy Lenny* and *Snowbound,* are survival stories. I am a survivor, have the survivor's mentality. Survivors take nothing for granted, expect the worst, persist. . . . It's an uncertain world. We all live in the shadow of a holocaust so vast it's beyond our powers to comprehend. There is no end to uncertainty, especially for the young. What if . . .? What will I do . . .? Will I be ready? I write my stories with the hope that they have something to say to young readers about the qualities needed to live today—indeed, to live in any time.

Bibliography

1971   *Guy Lenny*
1973   *Snowbound*
1974   *The Dollar Man*
1974   *The Solid Gold Kid* (with Norma Fox Mazer)
1978   *The War on Villa Street*
1979   *The Last Mission*
1981   *The Island Keeper*
1981   *I Love You, Stupid!*
1984   *Hey, Kid! Does She Love Me?*
1985   *When the Phone Rang*
1986   *Cave Under the City*
1987   *The Girl of His Dreams*
1988   *City Light*
1989   *Heartbeat* (with Norma Fox Mazer)

Norma Fox Mazer

A strong, clear memory of myself at the age of thirteen: I'm at an adult gathering, sitting well back in a big side-winged leather chair, feeling hidden, unseen, almost invisible. My favorite state. I can watch, think, observe. Maybe that's the exact moment when I come to the amazing conclusion that adults are just like us, the kids, only taller, louder, pushier. I'm already making up stories about me, my sisters, my friends. Now I can make up stories about them, too, because now I understand.

I was a middle sister in a three-sister sandwich. On one side was my younger sister, blonde, high-spirited, sassy. Asked how she got that noseful of cute little freckles, she said, "My mother left me out in the rain and I rusted." My uncle called her Dynamite. On the other side was my beautiful older sister, who was also smart (always on the Honor Roll, won oratorical contests) and good (never forgot my mother's birthday, made breakfast so Mother could sleep later). As for me, the one in the middle, the filling in the sandwich, they called me the selfish one (always thinking about herself) or the faucet, since I was famous, but not admired, for my tears on every occasion.

All of this, and more, much more, has worked itself into my books and stories, but never in a strictly autobiographical way. Both the narrator and her dead sister in "Do You Really Think It's Fair?" are based on aspects of my younger sister. The feeling between the Pennoyer sisters, Jenny and Gail, in *A Figure of Speech* and *When We First Met* are drawn from my early relationship to my older sister. I went back to three sisters in the book of that title, *Three Sisters*. "Why Was Elana Crying?" was a fictional recreation of my own teary childhood. Somewhere, I am in everything I write, even a book like *Downtown*, which speaks through the voice of a boy.

I was born in New York City, but lived there only until I was four. I've used Glens Falls, where I grew up, as the setting (as much emotional/imaginative as literal) for stories such as "Dear Bill, Remember Me?," "Mimi the Fish," and "Do You Really Think It's Fair?"; and Syracuse, where I've lived most of my adult life, for novels like *Up in Seth's Room* and *Someone to Love*. But to give myself the freedom I need in writing, I've imagined/created a fictional place, Alliance, a northern New York State working-class cum college town. There, Jenny Pennoyer's life takes place and so do the lives of Ami, Mia, Bunny, and Emily from the "Name" books, as well as Rachel Cooper in *After the Rain*, and Sarabeth Silver in *Silver.*

Working-class towns, working-class families are important to me. They are the fabric against which my life was drawn. My father drove a delivery truck, my mother worked in clothing stores. Work and the need for work was a constant thread in our lives. And my parents sitting around and gabbing about the past, their relatives, and friends was another constant. I didn't recognize it then as storytelling. Today, with hindsight, I suppose that my insistent need to write, to tell stories, is directly related to those past moments.

Bibliography

1971	*I, Trissy*
1973	*A Figure of Speech*
1975	*Saturday, the Twelfth of October*
1976	*Dear Bill, Remember Me? and Other Stories*
1977	*The Solid Gold Kid* (with Harry Mazer)
1979	*Up in Seth's Room*
1980	*Mrs. Fish, Ape, and Me, the Dump Queen*
1981	*Taking Terri Mueller*
1982	*Summer Girls, Love Boys and Other Stories*
1982	*When We First Met*
1983	*Someone to Love*
1984	*Supergirl*
1984	*Downtown*
1986	*Three Sisters*
1986	*A, My Name is Ami*
1987	*B, My Name is Bunny*

1987   *After the Rain*
1988   *Silver*
1989   *Heartbeat* (with Harry Mazer)
1989   *Waltzing on Water, Poems by Women* (edited with Marjorie Lewis)

Gloria D. Miklowitz

I grew up in New York, in Neil Simon's town—Brighton Beach—a community of intellectually curious, high-achieving Jewish kids whose parents expected them to become doctors and lawyers and never to forget those less fortunate than they. The middle child of five, I daydreamed so much I nearly flunked first grade, but once I learned to read, I devoured every book in the library, escaping from the noise and chaos of my large family to read in the locked bathroom, with my back against the tub, on the tile floor.

Graduating from the University of Michigan at the age of twenty, I went straight to *The New York Times* to apply for a job as reporter. After all, I'd been a reporter on my high school and college newspapers, and what else could one do with a B.A. in English? Not much, it seemed. I worked as secretary to the production manager at Bantam Books for seven months, then married and left New York for the West.

For five years, before my first son was born, I worked for the Navy Department in Pasadena as a scriptwriter of documentary films, on subjects for which I had no technical background—rockets and torpedoes. There I learned three valuable lessons: write visually, write clearly, and make every word count.

When my second son was born, I left the navy to be a full-time mother and began reading picture books to the children in order to sit down a few minutes each day. After reading hundreds of books aloud, I tried writing one and entered *Barefoot Boy* in Follett's Beginning-to-Read contest. Miraculously, the book sold and is still in print. As my children aged, so did the audience for the books I wrote. By the time my sons reached college I'd found the age I most enjoyed writing for—the young adult.

From the first, the novels I've written have been a way to find out *how I feel* about an issue or to try to understand something. Thus, when writing *Close to the Edge*, I was searching for my own answer to "why go on?"; in *The Emerson High Vigilantes*, I wondered if, legality aside, people *could* take the law into their own hands without going too far. In *The War Between the Classes* I wanted to explore the class system and its defects. In *After the Bomb* and its sequel I hoped to turn readers into activists against nuclear war and to make a hero of Philip, the protagonist, modeled after my own son who, as a teenager, seemed so inept and insecure.

I can't imagine a happier way to live than to write what I want, for whom I want, when I want. And to see some of my characters come to life on the TV screen in three award-winning school-break specials. But the best reward comes from my readers, especially those touched in some special way—such as the girl who wrote, after reading *Close to the Edge*, "You may have saved a life . . . mine."

Bibliography

Books for Young Adults

1973	*Turning Off*
1974	*A Time to Hurt, A Time to Heal*
1977	*Runaway*
1977	*Unwed Mother*
1977	*Paramedic Emergency*
1979	*Did You Hear What Happened to Andrea?*
1980	*The Love Bombers*
1982	*Before Love*
1983	*Carrie Loves Superman*
1983	*Close to the Edge*
1983	*The Day the Senior Class Got Married*
1985	*After the Bomb*
1985	*The War Between the Classes*
1986	*Love Story, Take Three*
1987	*After the Bomb, Week One*
1987	*Secrets Not Meant to be Kept*
1987	*Goodbye Tomorrow*
1988	*The Emerson High Vigilantes*
1989	*Anything to Win*

1989   *Suddenly Super Rich*

Books for Younger Readers

1964   *Barefoot Boy*
1977   *Ghastly Ghostly Riddles*

Nicholasa Mohr

F rom the moment my mother handed me some scrap paper, a pencil, and a few crayons, I decided that by making pictures and writing letters I could create my own world, like "magic." In the small, crowded apartment I shared with my large family (six older brothers, parents, aunt, and a boy cousin), "making magic" permitted me all the space and freedom my imagination could handle.

I was born in the urban village in the heart of New York City's Manhattan known as "El Barrio," meaning "the neighborhood." Also known as Spanish Harlem, it is the oldest Spanish-speaking community in the city. My parents had migrated with four small children from the island of Puerto Rico before the Second World War. Like many other strangers preceding them, they hoped that with hard work and opportunity they too could offer their children that good life known as the American Dream. Subsequently three more children were born, of which I was the youngest and only daughter.

We moved to the Bronx, where I spent most of my formative years. Through the loss of my parents and separation from my family in my early teens, I continued to rely on my ability to draw and to tell stories. After high school, I enrolled in the Art Students League and pursued my career as a fine artist. I studied in the Taller de Graficos in Mexico City, returned, and continued to study at the Brooklyn Museum Art School, the New School for Social Research, and the Pratt Center for Printmaking. I got married and had two sons, David and Jason. All of this time I worked and exhibited my prints and paintings in New York City galleries, and had my own studio as well as an art agent representing me. In 1972 when I was asked to do a book jacket for Harper and Row, I showed them fifty pages of vignettes I had written dealing with my childhood. The result was a contract and my first book. *Nilda* was published in 1973. I also did the book jacket and eight illustrations for *Nilda*.

What I thought would have been a temporary diversion (I assumed I'd return to visual art and be done with this business of writing!) turned out to be my new focus in life. Writing satisfied and fulfilled my needs to communicate in a way I had not experienced as a visual artist. *Nilda* is the most autobiographical of my books, not so much in fact (it takes place during the Second World War) but in feeling and circumstances. This was followed by *El Bronx Remembered*, a collection of short stories and a novella dealing with the decade of the promised future for Puerto Rican immigrants, 1946–1956. My next book was *In Nueva York*, a collection of inter-related stories about the Hispanic community in New York City's Lower East Side, during the end of the Vietnam War. *Felita*, a novel for younger children, is about contemporary times. It shows how a family is forced out of an all-white neighborhood and back to their barrio, and how in spite of this setback and humiliation, they pull together and continue to build a future for themselves. *Rituals of Survival*, an adult book, is a collection of stories about the struggles and courage of Puerto Rican women. This was followed by *Going Home*, a sequel to *Felita*. In this novel, Felita visits Puerto Rico to discover that she is seen as an outsider, a *gringa*, and she must deal with her identity. I have recently completed two plays and an original fairy tale. In celebration of my work, the State University of New York at Albany has awarded me an honorary Doctor of Letters degree.

Growing up, I had never seen or read *any book* that included Puerto Ricans (or Hispanics, for that matter) as citizens who worked hard and contributed to this nation. In American letters, we were *invisible*. Writing has given me the opportunity to establish my own sense of history and existence as a Puerto Rican woman in the literature of these United States. I know that even if I had been born rich, and white Anglo-Saxon Protestant, I would still be doing creative work . . . i.e., visual art and writing. However, because of who I am, I feel blessed by the work I do, for it permits me to use my imagination and continue to "make magic." With this magic, I can recreate those deepest of personal memories as well as validate and celebrate my heritage and my future.

Bibliography

1973   *Nilda*
1975   *El Bronx Remembered*
1977   *In Nueva York*
1979   *Felita*
1985   *Rituals of Survival: A Woman's Portfolio*
1986   *Going Home*

Walter Dean Myers

PHOTO: DAVID GODLIS

The real name is Walter Milton Myers. I was born in August 1937, in Martinsburg, West Virginia. The whole town is about ten square blocks, or smaller than the Harlem community in which I was raised. The trip to Harlem from Martinsburg was precipitated by the death of my mother when I was two.

Being raised Black in America has been the major influence in my life. First I had to figure out whether being Black was a good or bad thing. This is no mean trick when all of the heroes I was presented with were White. Finally I decided that being Black was at least okay.

The next problem was to figure out what being Black meant. Did it mean that I was a good athlete? Could I "naturally" sing and dance well? Was I sexually wonderful? The only thing I knew for certain was that I wanted to be like everyone else. To an extent I was like everyone else. I wore the same kind of clothes, the same brand of sneakers, went to the same schools. Oh, I did read more than some of my friends, but that didn't really count.

When I reached fifteen I had my first crises. Sorry, that's CRISES. The world didn't understand me. My folks didn't understand me. And no one seemed to understand the important things in life. Except me. I knew it all. I remember being relieved that at least someone knew what it was all about.

My foster father was a wonderful man. He gave me the most precious gift any father could give to a son. He loved me. He did it without articulating the nuances, and without really understanding the kind of person he was allowing me to be.

My foster mother understood the value of education, even though neither she nor my father had more than a rudimentary education. She also understood the value of story, how it could serve as a refuge for people, like us, who couldn't afford the finer things in life, or even all of what came to be the everyday things.

I've always been a bit uneasy about my lack of formal education. I was a good reader, and I took to stories to find my true identity. Could I have been an enchanted prince? Although the idea seems odd now, it certainly seemed better than being the poor child of a janitor when I was in my preteen period.

Langston Hughes lived a few blocks away. It was my discovery of Hughes that allowed my first efforts at writing to assume a new posture, one that said I could write about poor people in general, and poor Black people in particular. Wonderful.

Writing, being a writer, is wonderful. I love it more than anything else in the world. I think it's God's gift to me, and I would like to be remembered as giving something back to the world.

What I do now is to rediscover my life, in bits and pieces, and write about the wonderment of the rediscovery so that others might share. There are so many parts I haven't written about yet, but which I will come to soon. I hope.

Bibliography

Books for Young Adults

1975	*Fast Sam, Cool Clyde, and Stuff*
1977	*Brainstorm*
1977	*Mojo and the Russians*
1977	*Victory for Jamie*
1978	*It Ain't All for Nothin'*
1981	*Hoops*
1981	*The Legend of Tarik*
1982	*Won't Know Till I Get There*
1983	*The Nicholas Factor*
1983	*Tales of a Dead King*
1984	*The Outside Shot*
1984	*Motown and Didi: A Love Story*
1986	*Sweet Illusions*
1986	*Crystal*
1988	*Fallen Angels*
1988	*Scorpions*
1989	*Me, Mop, and the Moondance Kid*

Books for Younger Readers

1969	*Where Does the Day Go?*, illus. by Leo Carty
1972	*The Dancers*, illus. by Anne Rockwell
1972	*The Dragon Takes a Wife*, illus. by Ann Grifalconi
1974	*Fly, Jimmy, Fly!*, illus. by Moneta Barnett
1980	*The Golden Serpent*, illus. by Alice and Martin Provensen
1980	*The Black Pearl and the Ghost*, illus. by Robert Quackenbush
1984	*Mr. Monkey and the Gotcha Bird*, illus. by Leslie Morill

Series

1985–86	*Arrow*

Nonfiction for Young Readers

1975	*The World of Work*
1976	*Social Welfare, A First Book*

Joan Lowery Nixon

I took a fascinatingly introspective course a few years ago, when "getting in touch with yourself" became popular. Our assignment in one session was to close our eyes, picture ourselves at the age of ten, and report to these children of our pasts about the progress we'd made since that time.

It wasn't hard to remember how I'd looked when I was ten: long "sausage" curls, a barrette slipping out of place, wirerimmed glasses sliding on my nose, perpetually skinned knees from roller-skating, and a book always in my hands. I grinned at this little Joan Marie, gave her a hug, and said, "Hey, kid! You did it!" because ever since my earliest recollections, I knew absolutely and positively that someday I was going to be a writer.

I was born in Los Angeles and grew up in Hollywood. I graduated from the University of Southern California with a degree in journalism, but I found myself teaching kindergarten because no one wanted to hire inexperienced journalists and the city of Los Angeles desperately needed teachers. I enjoyed teaching so much I went to night classes at California State College and obtained a credential in elementary education.

From the time I was seventeen I wrote nonfiction freelance articles for magazines, but in 1961, the year after my husband, my four children, and I had moved to Corpus Christi, Texas (we now live in Houston), I attended my first writers' conference. I told my family I'd been interested in what two authors had said about writing for children and might give it a try. My two eldest, Kathy and Maureen, put their heads together, came to me, and said, "If you're going to write for children, you have to write a book, it has to be a mystery, and you have to put us in it."

To please them I did, and in 1964 my first book for children, *The Mystery of Hurricane Castle*, was published. I was hooked and have written for children ever since. Although I enjoy writing all types of stories for all ages, I've been particularly fond of the mystery format—especially for young adult readers. Its longer length gives me more space in which to develop the story and more opportunity to delve deeply into characterizations. I write with two story lines, intertwining them. My main character has both a personal problem and a mystery to solve.

I've branched out from the mystery in other novels for young adults, such as the historical stories in *The Orphan Train Quartet* and in the *Hollywood Daughters* trilogy. The first book of *Hollywood Daughters* takes place in Hollywood in early 1942, and the teenaged main character is mother to the teen who stars in the second book, and grandmother to the teen in the third. (A little of my own life is in the first story, so what a shock it was when my editor said, "Remember, to today's kids this is *historical* fiction.")

In my opinion, writing is the best job in the world. It's not surprising. I always knew it would be.

Bibliography

Books for Young Adults

1979   *The Kidnapping of Christina Lattimore*
1980   *The Seance*
1982   *The Specter*
1983   *A Deadly Game of Magic*
1984   *The Ghosts of Now*
1985   *The Stalker*
1986   *The Other Side of Dark*
1987   *The Dark and Deadly Pool*
1988   *Secret, Silent Screams*
1989   *Island of Dangerous Dreams*
1989   *Shadows of Fear*
1990   *Hollywood Daughters: A Trilogy*

Series

1987–89   *The Orphan Train Quartet (A Family Apart, Caught in the Act, In the Face of Danger, A Place to Belong)*

Other Books

Scott O'Dell

PHOTO: JIM KALETT

Los Angeles was a frontier town when I was born there. It had more horses than automobiles and more jackrabbits than people. The first sound I remember was a wildcat scratching on the roof of our house.

We moved a lot, but never far. To San Pedro, which was part of Los Angeles, and Rattlesnake Island, across the bay from San Pedro, where three-masted ships sailed by. The memory of my years at San Pedro and Dead Man's Island, where, with other boys my age, I voyaged out on summer mornings in search of adventure, would flesh out *Island of the Blue Dolphins*, the true story of Karana, the Indian girl who lived alone on a California island for eighteen years.

I graduated from Polytechnic High School in Long Beach, California, the brightest boy—my teachers said—they'd ever had or hoped to have. I thought so, too. However, when I went to college I found to my great surprise that I was not the brightest young man in the world. Indeed, I found that most of my classmates were brighter than I was. Things had been so easy in elementary and high school, I hadn't needed to study. What's more, I didn't know how. That is why I wandered around from school to school—from Occidental College to the University of Wisconsin, to the University of Rome, to Stanford.

Always, I knew I would be a writer. But along the way I spent several years in Hollywood, working in the motion picture industry. When the second company of *Ben Hur* (the silent version, starring Ramon Navarro) went to Italy, I went along as cameraman, carrying the first technicolor camera, a prototype made by hand at MIT. We shot thousands of feet of film in Rome, just as the company before us had done. But none of it was ever used. After months of hard work, surprises, and disasters, the company went back to the United States, and the film was shot on the back lots in Hollywood.

My first novels were not for young people. It was not until 1960, twenty-six years after my first novel for adults was published, that I wrote a book for young children. It was *Island of the Blue Dolphins*, a story that began in anger—anger at the hunters who came into the mountains near Julian, where I lived, killing everything that could walk or creep or fly. Through that book I tried to convey a simple, but profound, message: forgive your enemies and have respect for life—all life.

Whether remembered or imagined, all of my stories are in a certain sense written not for children but for myself, out of a personal need. If children or young adults enjoy them, it's because the stories exist in the emotional area we share.

For the past thirteen years, I've lived in the wilds of Westchester County, New York, about fifty miles north of Manhattan. My house is on the shore of a lake, surrounded by a forest of oak and maple and birch, where geese glide on the water, cardinals breakfast beside us, raccoons call each night for dinner, and deer dine on our shrubs and flowers and bed down in the orchard grass. Yesterday morning we were visited by a great blue heron, who fished patiently for an hour. All this wildlife keeps my dog, a Siberian husky who roams through the pages of *Black Star, Bright Dawn*, in a continual state of excitement.

Bibliography

1960   *Island of the Blue Dolphins*
1966   *The King's Fifth*
1967   *The Black Pearl*
1968   *The Dark Canoe*
1968   *Journey to Jericho*
1970   *Sing Down the Moon*
1973   *The Cruise of the Arctic Star*
1974   *Child of Fire*
1975   *The Hawk That Dare Not Hunt By Day*
1976   *The 290*
1976   *Carlota*
1978   *Kathleen, Please Come Home*
1979   *The Captive*
1980   *Sara Bishop*

Zibby Oneal

PHOTO: STEPHEN BLOS

My father was a Sunday painter. My mother was in love with words. What I remember best about our house is the stacks of books and the smell of oil paint.

For a time in my childhood I couldn't decide which way to go—would I write or would I paint?—but by the time I was ten or so, I'd settled on writing. I'd sit out under the elm tree in our backyard in Omaha, Nebraska, and make up stories while my sister and her friends did things like roller-skate. I was a solitary child—no doubt about it—but no one ever worried over that. My parents understood that a writer needed solitude.

My earliest stories were always set in places I had never been—Bangkok, for instance, or Paris, or Tahiti. But, strangely enough, the first book I wrote as an adult—a book called *War Work*—was set squarely in Omaha, Nebraska, and some of it took place beneath an elm tree.

Maybe this isn't really so strange. I think that sooner or later most writers return in some way to what they know best. Places I've lived or that I have visited many times provide the settings for all the books I write now. I seem most comfortable settling my characters into familiar landscapes where the street corners, the bus stops, even the trees and weeds and angles of light, are well known to me.

A Formal Feeling takes place in a university town much like Ann Arbor, Michigan, where I live now. *In Summer Light* is set on the island of Martha's Vineyard, where my husband and I and our two children have spent many summers. *The Language of Goldfish* takes place in the Chicago suburb where my husband grew up. One day, I suspect, I will write a story set in the California hills near Stanford University, where I spent my college years.

157

But regardless of where any new story takes place, it is almost certain to be about a family, just as my other books have been. Families fascinate me. No matter what I set out to write, before long I have created another one, and I find that it is the relationships within that family that interest me most.

We become ourselves because of our families—or perhaps in spite of them—but surely they are where we have to start when we set forth to discover our own identities. My characters start out on such voyages of discovery only to find—as I did—that the real discoveries begin at home.

Long ago, pondering my choices under that elm tree, I decided that I would write, but I never quite gave up on art. I think this is why there are so many artists in the books I write and why there is such a lot about color and light. This is a way for me to join words and paint, to bring together those parts of myself that became parts so many years ago, in my family, in that first important place.

From time to time I teach a course in creative writing at the University of Michigan. I advise my students to write about those things they know best and feel most deeply—to trust, in other words, to their own experience. But I cannot take credit for this advice. It was given to me by my parents. Each of them told me at one time or another that if I'd ever stop writing about Bangkok and Tahiti I might get somewhere someday.

Bibliography

Books for Young Adults

1980   *The Language of Goldfish*
1982   *A Formal Feeling*
1985   *In Summer Light*

Other Books

1971   *War Work*
1972   *The Improbable Adventures of Marvelous O'Hara Soapstone*
1978   *Turtle and Snail*
1985   *Maude and Walter*
1985   *Grandma Moses: Painter of Rural America*
1989   *Lila's Story*

Katherine Paterson

PHOTO: JILL PATON WALSH

I was born in Qing Jiang, China, on Halloween Day, 1932, the middle of five children of missionary parents named Womeldorf. Our mother read to us from infancy, and long before I entered first grade I had taught myself to read because I could not bear not being able to. I began to write soon after, but school ruined my style while it sought vainly to correct my spelling. So by the time I was eight, I was writing imitations of *Elsie Dinsmore,* which were mercifully lost during the fifteen moves that my family made between my fourth and eighteenth years.

I received an A.B. in English Literature from King College in Bristol, Tennessee, a tiny Presbyterian college which was poor in everything except wise and caring professors who gave me Shakespeare and John Donne and Gerard Manley Hopkins.

I eventually earned two master's degrees, one from the Presbyterian School of Christian Education in Richmond, Virginia, and another from Union Theological Seminary in New York City. During this span of years, I also taught sixth grade in Lovettsville, Virginia, and spent four years as a missionary to Japan under the Presbyterian Church.

In 1962, I met and married John Barstow Paterson, who was and still is a Presbyterian minister. John and I have four children, Elizabeth PoLin, John Jr., David Lord, and Mary Katherine Nah-he-sah-pe-chc-a. Lin was born in Hong Kong in 1962 and came to us in 1964, six months after John was born. David was born in 1966, and two years later we adopted Mary, a five-month-old Apache-Kiowan. Between 1964 and 1973, I mostly cooked, cleaned, diapered, and—whenever I could—read, either aloud or to myself, and wrote, publishing almost nothing.

My first novel was written a chapter a week for an adult education class in 1968–69 and finally published in 1973. It and the two following novels are all set in feudal Japan and reflect my love for that country and my fascination with its history.

I moved to the setting of my first year of teaching when, after the death of David's closest friend, I wrote *Bridge to Terabithia*. *The Great Gilly Hopkins* was set in Takoma Park, where we lived for thirteen years, far longer than I have ever lived anywhere else in my nomadic life. Takoma Park is about an hour from the Chesapeake Bay, which became the setting for *Jacob Have I Loved*. That book wasn't finished until after we had moved to Norfolk, Virginia, at the other end of the bay.

I returned to China to smell and see and listen so that I could write *Rebels of the Heavenly Kingdom*. I love to write historical fiction, though the rewards are few. The vagaries of fame led me to write *Come Sing, Jimmy Jo;* and *Park's Quest* grew out of my participation in the National Women's Conference to Prevent Nuclear War and my friendship with a family whose eldest son had died in Vietnam. By the time it was finished, our children had grown and we had moved to Vermont.

People have asked me through the years whether, when my children left home, I would begin to write adult fiction. Why should I want to? It's a joy to write for people who are eager to enter imaginatively into a book, who often reread a book they love, and who always hope it will be the best they've ever read.

Bibliography

Books for Young Adults

1973   *The Sign of the Chrysanthemum*
1974   *Of Nightingales that Weep*
1976   *The Master Puppeteer*
1977   *Bridge to Terabithia*
1978   *The Great Gilly Hopkins*
1979   *Angels and Other Strangers*
1980   *Jacob Have I Loved*
1983   *Rebels of the Heavenly Kingdom*
1985   *Come Sing, Jimmy Jo*
1986   *Consider the Lilies* (with John Paterson)
1988   *Park's Quest*

Other Books

1981   *The Crane Wife* (translation from the Japanese)
1981   *Gates of Excellence*
1987   *The Tongue-Cut Sparrow* (translation from the Japanese)
1989   *The Spying Heart*

Gary Paulsen

Born May 17, 1939; married to a lady named Ruth, who is an artist; have one son named James; and used to participate (as a hobby) in dogsledding—I ran distance races, five hundred to a thousand miles. Have twice run in the Iditarod trans-Alaskan race from Anchorage to Nome.

Two hundred articles and short stories published in many of the national magazines. Two produced plays; done political and press writing; have worked on setting one novel to dance (*Dancing Carl*), which was produced and aired on Minnesota Public Television; have taught at the University of Colorado and Bemidji State College; won various awards; done some acting; some living, but mostly writing. Just writing. Currently at work on finishing *The Winter Stories* for Orchard Press and the screenplay for *Hatchet*; also continuing work on a series of short stories called *The Madonna,* a study of the relationship between men and the women who raise them.

Bibliography

Books for Young Adults

1968	*Mr. Tucket*
1976	*Winterkill*
1978	*The Foxman*
1978	*Tiltawhirl John*
1980	*The Night the White Deer Died*
1980	*Spitball Gang*
1983	*Popcorn Days and Buttermilk Nights*
1983	*Dancing Carl*

1984	*Tracker*
1986	*Dogsong*
1986	*Sentries*
1987	*Hatchet*
1987	*The Crossing*
1988	*The Island*
1988	*The Voyage of the Frog*
1989	*The Boy Who Owned the School*
1989	*The Winter Stories*

Books for Younger Readers

1976	*The Golden Stick*
1977	*The Curse of the Cobra*
1977	*CB Radio Caper*

Juvenile Nonfiction

1976	*Real Animals: The Small Ones*
1976	*Real Animals: The Grass Eaters*
1976	*The Man Who Climbed the Mountain*
1977	*Airlines*
1977	*Farms—A Career Profile*
1979	*Sailing*
1979	*Canoeing, Kayaking, Rafting*
1980	*Hiking and Backpacking*
1981	*Television and Movie Animals*

Series

1976–78	*Sports Humor—[Baseball, Basketball, Hockey, Football . . .]*

Books for Adults

1975	*The Implosion Effect*
1976	*CB Jockey*
1977	*The Death Specialists*
1981	*Meteorite—Track 291*
1981	*Compkill*
1981	*Clutterkill*
1982	*The Sweeper*
1984	*The Meatgrinder*
1988	*Murphy's Gold*

Adult Nonfiction

Richard Peck

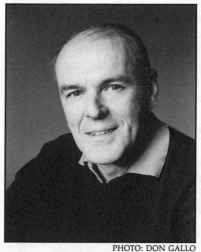

PHOTO: DON GALLO

I grew up in Decatur, Illinois, a middle-American town with plenty of local color. Long after, it became the Dunthorpe of *Dreamland Lake* and *Representing Super Doll.* The town as it might have been back at the turn of the century became the Bluff City of the four comic novels starring Blossom Culp and AA.

When I was in grade school, World War II was raging, and so our teachers taught from maps. We not only learned geography, but we also learned we weren't the center of the world. In junior high, a teacher told me that Latin was not an elective, and I believed her. That was fortunate because I couldn't have become a writer without it. Back there before social studies, our high school teachers taught survey courses in European and American history that might be hard to find in colleges today. My schooling laid the groundwork for a novelist: history, Latin, and geography—something to say, how to say it, and somewhere to set the story.

I went to college in England, at Exeter University, where I learned that even English is a foreign language. I returned to DePauw University in Greencastle, Indiana, to take education courses for a teaching credential. However, my first opportunity to use a college degree came in the army. There I first learned the advantage of majoring in English because I devised a good, sitting-down job as a ghost writer of sermons for chaplains, all denominations. A lot of people brought their problems to the chaplain's office, and those problems still surface in my novels.

When I became a teacher, it was my students who really made a writer out of me. High school students at Glenbrook North High School in Illinois introduced me to the world of suburbia and of coming of age there. In time, that resulted in at least three novels—

Close Enough to Touch, Remembering the Good Times, and a satire called *Secrets of the Shopping Mall.* Junior high students in New York taught me the novelist's most important lesson: that a novel must entertain first before it can do anything else. That's not the sort of thing you learn by majoring in English.

On May 24, 1971, I quit teaching in order to write to the young readers I'd met in my classrooms. It was a memorable date; you always remember the day you turned in your tenure. That first novel was *Don't Look and It Won't Hurt.* These days, amazingly, I have readers who are younger than that book.

My chief inspiration now comes from the letters young readers send back to a writer. Some of them want to become writers themselves. There is no foolproof formula, but they want one. And so I send them this: If you want to be a writer,

1. Learn five new words a day, keep a list, and use the words.
2. Take Latin, for the framework.
3. Since novels are never about ordinary people, get acquainted with people in your school who aren't full-time conformists.

Bibliography

Books for Young Adults

1972	*Don't Look and It Won't Hurt*
1973	*Dreamland Lake*
1973	*Through a Brief Darkness*
1974	*Representing Super Doll*
1975	*The Ghost Belonged to Me*
1976	*Are You in the House Alone?*
1977	*Ghosts I Have Been*
1978	*Father Figure*
1979	*Secrets of the Shopping Mall*
1981	*Close Enough to Touch*
1983	*The Dreadful Future of Blossom Culp*
1985	*Remembering the Good Times*
1986	*Blossom Culp and the Sleep of Death*
1987	*Princess Ashley*
1988	*Those Summer Girls I Never Met*

Other Books

| 1966 | *Edge of Awareness: Twenty-five Contemporary Essays* (editor, with Ned E. Hoopes) |

1970	*Sounds and Silences: Poetry for Now* (editor)
1971	*Mindscapes: Poems for the Real World* (editor)
1973	*Leap into Reality: Essays for Now* (editor)
1976	*Pictures That Storm Inside My Head: Poems for the Inner You* (editor)
1977	*Monster Night at Grandma's House*, illus. by Don Freeman
1980	*Amanda/Miranda*
1981	*New York Time*
1983	*This Family of Women*

Robert Newton Peck

Better known as Rob. Best known as Soup's best pal. Raised on a Vermont farm; attended a one-room school; dropped out of high school; served overseas in World War II as a machine-gunner, 88th Infantry; has commendation from General Mark Clark.

Author of forty-six books, one hundred poems, thirty-five songs (words and music), creator of three TV specials, winner of the Mark Twain Award, ragtime piano player, stand-up comic, lousy dancer, enthusiastic yet untalented athlete, habitual show-off. Loves kids, reveres teachers but abhors unions, has never used a four-letter word in forty-six books yet does use them on a golf course.

Rob is 6'4" tall, weighs two hundred pounds, gave up tobacco, drinks scotch and soda, shoots pool, plays poker, can windsurf and jet-ski, is an expert snow skier, and is afraid to skydive. Reluctant to usher in church when other three ushers are five feet tall. Hasn't dropped the collection plate in almost a year. Preached one sermon. In college was preministerial student whose goal was to become the first Protestant Pope. Was class president at Cornell Law School and flunked out with the lowest scholastic average ever recorded in Ithaca, New York.

Now owns publishing company, Peck Press. Loves to do a gig at conferences of writers, teachers, librarians. Imagines that Hell is an endless awards banquet. Avoids doctors, lawyers, clergymen, judges, politicians, bureaucrats, lobbyists, and high school principals who are former football coaches.

Dislikes macho men and feminist women. Instead, prefers ladies and gentlemen.

Answers one hundred letters every week, estimates that soon he'll have written notes to 100,000 kids.

168

In 1958 married a librarian (TV's Mr. Rogers was best man). Still married . . . despite his snoring, football-watching, and eating Ritz crackers in bed. Two handsome children: Christopher Haven Peck, age twenty-one, a dean's-list junior at Flagler College, cheerleader, industrial-strength weightlifter, looks (and often smells) like Conan's horse. Anne Houston Peck, age seventeen, sings, dances, plays piano, telephones, majoring in boys and mascara. Bright mind, perfect figure, dismal student. Anne is to academics what Bella Abzug is to pole-vaulting. A bud still to blossom.

Rob teaches a course—"How to Write a Book"—every autumn. Rents a posh hotel suite complete with piano and a bar. Many writers take it more than once, because Rob is so unlike creative-writing college profs who couldn't write a suicide note.

RNP is a cornball, flag-waving, redneck patriot who loves America and respects the thinking of Americans who do hard physical work. He writes about them, folks who stand in dirt and look up at rainbows.

His address: 500 Sweetwater Club Circle
Longwood, Florida 32779
His phone: (407) 788-3456
Call up and say howdy.

Bibliography

Books for Children and Young Adults

1973	*A Day No Pigs Would Die*
1973	*Path of Hunters*
1973	*Millie's Boy*
1974	*Soup*
1975	*Fawn*
1975	*Wild Cat*
1975	*Bee Tree* (poems)
1975	*Soup and Me*
1976	*Hamilton*
1976	*Hang for Treason*
1976	*Rabbits and Redcoats*
1977	*Trig*
1977	*Last Sunday*
1977	*The King's Iron*
1977	*Patooie*

Stella Pevsner

PHOTO: TOM FEZZEY

Children sometimes ask if I wanted to be a writer when I was young. Occasionally I'll say, "No, I really wanted to be a tap dancer." Or sometimes, "No, an actress." Or, "a singer." I believed any of these vocations would provide a direct route to joy, satisfaction, and fame beyond measure. To hone my incipient talents I would sometimes, on winter evenings, coerce my brothers into playing "show," with a rolled-up rug to mark the footlight area of the stage. I would sing and tap-dance and ignore their rude remarks. It was good practice for rejection slips that would come my way in the future, as they do to most beginning writers.

Eventually, I realized that the performing arts could survive without me, to their probable benefit. Anyway, I was going to be an artist. I thought. It wasn't until high school that I took an interest in writing, and that was because one of the teachers asked me to write a humor column for the school magazine. I told him I didn't know how, so he loaned me a book of essays by Thurber and others and said, "Go to it." I did, and loved the experience. Later on I took an elective creative writing class and it was great, but it never occurred to me that some day I could be a writer. No one actually wrote for a living. No one that I or anyone in my hometown of Lincoln, Illinois, knew. Writers either lived somewhere else in luxurious villas or were dead, like Shakespeare.

During all those growing-up years I read. I read when I was supposed to be dusting the living room; I read when I was supposed to be paying attention in class; I read walking back and forth from school. Reading was a way of living other lives. It was compensation for being born in one time period, in one place, with one family. Books let me roam everywhere, experience the improbable,

171

become confidante of many. Still, I was a restless child, a born vagabond. I never saw a train or plane without wishing I were on it, going somewhere spectacular. This desire for travel is something I've never outgrown. Writing has helped make it happen.

In my single years I worked as a copywriter and also a publicist for various Chicago ad agencies. Later on, with marriage and suburban life and babies, I did a bit of freelancing here and there. Mostly, I did the PTA thing, the Fun Fair thing, the Room Mother thing, and was the mover and shaker behind kid birthday parties that seemed to occur as often as phases of the moon. But the thought always lurked, *This is just a role I'm playing. People don't realize I'm really a writer.*

One day a friend from my ad agency days invited me to a writers' group session in a distant suburb. It was wonderful to meet other people who thought writing was a sensible thing to do ... not frivolous at all. I kept going, began to write regularly, and eventually got interested in children's books. After my first one was published in 1968, I did another and another. It opened up a whole new, great kind of world. I can live an adult life and yet keep in touch with childhood. And there, I've led many lives.

Bibliography

Books for Young Adults

1978	*And You Give Me a Pain, Elaine*
1980	*Cute Is a Four-Letter Word*
1981	*I'll Always Remember You ... Maybe*
1983	*Lindsay, Lindsay, Fly Away Home*
1987	*Sister of the Quints*
1989	*How Could You Do It, Diane?*

Other Books

1969	*Break a Leg!*
1971	*Footsteps on the Stairs*
1973	*Call Me Heller, That's My Name*
1975	*A Smart Kid Like You*
1977	*Keep Stompin' Till the Music Stops*
1985	*Me, My Goat, and My Sister's Wedding*

Susan Beth Pfeffer

PHOTO: DONAL HOLWAY

I am a quintessential baby boomer, born in 1948, high school class of '65, graduated college in '69. The dream childhood of the fifties was mine—the house in the suburbs (Woodmere, Long Island), the first TV on the block, a summer home in the Catskills, schools that assumed students would do well, a guaranteed college education.

But my family bore little resemblance to those on TV, no talking horses for one thing. My father is a constitutional lawyer, my mother a secretary, and my older brother a genius, and none of them quite understood that the fifties were supposed to be a decade of conservative conformity. So I was a bit more prepared for the sixties than many other people of my generation, and the various revolutions that took place then seemed perfectly reasonable to me.

I went to NYU because it had a film department, and I wanted to be a Great Film Director. The only thing that stopped me was a complete lack of talent. Good fortune stepped in, and my last semester in college I wrote my first book, *Just Morgan*. So I've been a writer my entire professional life, but I still go to the movies a lot.

Actually, except for that little burst of Great Film Director madness, I'd always wanted to be a writer. My father's first book had been published when I was six, and I still remember reading the title and dedication pages over and over, admiring the way the words Pfeffer and Susan looked in print. And if you're twenty when you write your first book, writing for teenagers makes perfect sense; you still are one. As it happens, I love writing for teenagers, so I stumbled onto the work that was ideal for me. Teenagers have such peculiar problems, although I must admit I saddle my characters with problems that would be peculiar to people of any age. I

173

like to create normal people and see how they'd behave in abnormal situations.

I live in Middletown, New York, for no particular reason except I like it, with my two cats, Louisa and Isaac. Neither one of them talks, but they both manage to make their needs known to me. When I'm not writing, I talk with my friends and family, bake chocolate chip cookies, watch endless amounts of TV, read too many magazines and not enough books, and shop. I radiate contentment, with cause.

Bibliography

Books for Young Adults

1970	*Just Morgan*
1972	*Better Than All Right*
1973	*Rainbows and Fireworks*
1974	*The Beauty Queen*
1974	*Whatever Words You Want to Hear*
1975	*Marly the Kid*
1979	*Starring Peter and Leigh*
1980	*About David*
1982	*A Matter of Principle*
1983	*Starting with Melodie*
1984	*Fantasy Summer*
1986	*Getting Even*
1987	*The Year without Michael*

Series

| 1985–86 | *Make Me a Star* |
| 1988–90 | *The Sebastian Sisters* |

Books for Younger Readers

1977	*Kid Power*
1980	*Just Between Us*
1981	*What Do You Do When Your Mouth Won't Open?*
1983	*Courage, Dana*
1984	*Kid Power Strikes Back*

1986   *The Friendship Pact*
1988   *Rewind to Yesterday*
1988   *Turning Thirteen*
1989   *Future Forward*
1989   *Dear Dad, Love Laurie*

Kin Platt

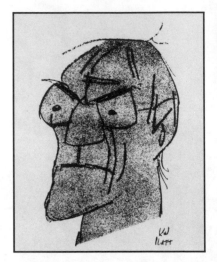

Born in New York City, I began my professional career in 1930 as theatrical and political caricaturist for the demised *Brooklyn Daily Eagle,* the *World-Telegram,* and other media. Later did cartoons and comic strips for advertising agencies, and sport cartoons for newspapers and magazines.

By 1936 I was writing radio comedy, *Stoopnagle and Bud* and *Jack Benny.* That led to Hollywood. Wrote the *National Biscuit Show* starring Helen Broderick and Victor Moore with a new singer from Texas, Mary Martin, still my friend, and Buddy Rogers and his orchestra. Wrote for most radio comics and lastly for Edgar Bergen. My flaring temper cost me too many shows and I returned to New York with wife and resumed cartooning. Wrote and drew thousands of comic books, created Supermouse, wrote many animated cartoon features.

World War II took me to China, Burma, and India with the air force. Did three years, won a Bronze Star and finally a Good Conduct medal, the last more difficult because my fights with the military bureaucracy were constantly getting me into trouble. They didn't like my lampooning the red tape with cartoons and skits.

Nineteen forty-six saw my release and my start with the *New York Herald Tribune* doing the comic strip *MR AND MRS,* created by Briggs and syndicated worldwide. Added *THE DUKE AND THE DUCHESS* and did both until the paper failed in 1963.

The Blue Man in 1961 for Harper Brothers was the beginning of my book career. *Big Max* was next. Then my important books for Chilton under John Marion—*The Boy Who Could Make Himself Disappear; Hey, Dummy;* and *Sinbad and Me,* the Edgar-winning best juvenile mystery of 1966. *Mystery of the Witch Who Wouldn't,* the second MWA award. *Chloris and the Creeps.* There were two Chloris sequels, *Freaks* and *Weirdos*. The third in the Sinbad series, *The Ghost of Hellsfire Street*. Another *Big Max* and, among the twenty or so others later, *The Ape Inside Me; Crocker; Brogg's Brain; Run for Your Life; Headman,* an ALA notable; *The Doomsday Gang; Dracula, Go Home; Frank and Stein and Me; Flames Going Out;* and *The Terrible Love Life of Dudley Cornflower.*

Meanwhile I had started my adult line with the Max Roper private-eye series, and the Molly Mellinger (pen name) book for Random House. My last published adult book was the Irish mystery *Murder in Rosslare.*

I've done about forty books and would have done many more but for differences with editors. They have the final word and at times where a compromise would have been best, I've resisted rather than tamper with my own best judgment. I've had bad editors and good ones but in the process have had to eat a lot of my books. It's always been a struggle having books done my way and is part of the game. They can break your heart if you let them, but if your work is good you must believe in it and be patient. But all in all, it's been memorable in many ways, and I've accomplished what I set out to do—write the very best books within my power.

Bibliography

Books for Young Adults

1966	*Sinbad and Me*
1968	*The Boy Who Could Make Himself Disappear*
1969	*Mystery of the Witch Who Wouldn't*
1971	*Hey, Dummy*
1974	*Chloris and the Creeps*
1975	*Chloris and the Freaks*
1975	*Headman*
1975	*Big Max and the Mystery of the Missing Moose*
1976	*The Terrible Love Life of Dudley Cornflower*
1977	*Run for Your Life*
1978	*Chloris and the Weirdos*
1978	*The Doomsday Gang*
1979	*The Ape Inside Me*
1979	*Dracula, Go Home*
1980	*The Ghost of Hellsfire Street*
1980	*Flames Going Out*

1981	*Brogg's Brain*
1982	*Frank and Stein and Me*
1983	*Crocker*

Books for Adults

1961	*The Blue Man*
1965	*Big Max*
1969	*Pandora*
1974	*A Pride of Women*
1980	*Dead as They Come* (as Molly Mellinger)
1986	*Murder in Rosslare*

Series

| 1970–present | *Max Roper, Private Detective* |
| 1974–76 | *Hitman* |

Marilyn Sachs

PHOTO: MORRIS SACHS

I became a writer because I had an older sister who wanted to be one. She seemed a glorious creature to me when I was a child, and I copied her shamelessly. Somewhere along the line, I began to see myself as a separate entity and to search for my own voice. Strangely enough, she never became a writer, but I did.

So it's hard for me to offer firm advice on who should or shouldn't go into writing. I do know that you need not be the smartest one in your class or the one who is the most fussed over. Sometimes a little neglect is a good thing. It took me ten years to get my first book published. I don't recommend waiting that long, but I certainly was deliriously happy when it was finally accepted, and determined that I wouldn't let the same thing happen for the second. Since then, 1964, I've had twenty-seven other books published.

I grew up poor and Jewish in the Bronx, New York City. Just about everybody on my street was poor, so it didn't seem anything special. There were no birds or trees on my street, but I didn't know I was deprived. My childhood was rich with the sounds, tastes, and color of New York City in the thirties and forties. Now I live with my family in San Francisco, and don't think I'd be happy living anywhere other than a large city.

The city was safe when I was a child, and my friends (when I had any) and I roamed all over the Bronx. Somewhere around the time I was eight or nine, I found my way to the Morrisania Branch of the New York Public Library, and that's where my training as a writer began.

I've always loved to read, and still do. Reading and writing, it seems to me, are two sides of the same coin. You can't really learn

179

to write well unless you learn how to tell a story, and you won't learn how to tell a story if you don't read.

I was a loser as a child—small, puny, cowardly, and a terrible liar. Lying is actually a good quality for prospective writers because writers deal with fantasy. We nibble at the truth, if there is such a thing, embroider it, make it worse, make it better, but above all try to make it interesting. Anybody can write, but the trick is to find people who want to read what you've written. Readers make writers.

Many of my books deal with losers because I was one as a child. *The Fat Girl* is about a fat girl; *Bus Ride* concerns a shy, funny-looking boy and an unpopular girl with acne; the main character in *Hello . . . Wrong Number* is a boy with a big nose; and *Underdog* has two losers—a neglected girl and a neglected dog.

There are many young people out in the world who perceive of themselves as losers. I think of them as I write and hope they will find in the books they read the same kind of comfort and hope I've always found in mine. Books can close doors as well as open them. Whenever the world grows too uncomfortable, I know I can always find a safe place in the right book.

I'm married to a sculptor and have a grown son, daughter, and a son-in-law. I love being a writer and can't think of anything else I'd rather be doing.

Bibliography

Books for Young Adults

1979	*A Summer's Lease*
1980	*Class Pictures*
1980	*Bus Ride*
1981	*Hello . . . Wrong Number*
1982	*Call Me Ruth*
1982	*Beach Towels*
1983	*Fourteen*
1985	*The Fat Girl*
1985	*Thunderbird*
1986	*Baby Sister*
1987	*Almost Fifteen*
1989	*Just Like a Friend*

Books for Younger Readers

1964	*Amy Moves In*
1965	*Laura's Luck*
1966	*Amy and Laura*
1968	*Veronica Ganz*
1969	*Peter and Veronica*
1970	*Marv*
1971	*The Bears' House*
1973	*The Truth about Mary Rose*
1973	*A Pocket Full of Seeds*
1976	*Dorrie's Book*
1976	*A December Tale*
1978	*A Secret Friend*
1985	*Underdog*
1987	*Fran Ellen's House*
1989	*Matt's Mitt and Fleet Footed Florence*

Nicole St. John (Norma Johnston)

TENDER VISIONS PHOTOGRAPHY STUDIO

W ho am I? I'm Nicole St. John, Norma Johnston, Lavinia Harris, Kate Chambers, Pamela Dryden, Catherine E. Chambers, Elizabeth Bolton, and Adrian Robert. I've written nearly ninety books so far. I'm an author, editor, ghostwriter, entrepreneur, actress, director, designer, stylist, retailer, teacher, counselor, and (as some critics have said, and I'm proud of it!) preacher. Those aren't just job labels; they're who I am, how I use the talents I've been given— because that we all *do* have talents of one kind or another, and a responsibility to use them for the common good, is one of the things I most surely believe.

All the pieces of my life have overlapped; everything comes round, not full circle, but in spirals. Everything hooks back onto the center, then spins out again. The circle of rocks on which my life is built are these: my grandmother, and the family heritage I was born into; books I've read or written; plays I've seen or been in or directed. Also my faith, and the church I became deeply involved in as a teenager—and my theatre training, for in a weird and wonderful way these two interpreted and illumined each other and all the rest.

The roots of my family tree stretch on my mother's side back to the Dutch Metselaars and Van Zandts who colonized New Amsterdam in 1632 and to the Pierces from Dorsetshire, England, who came to Dorchester, Massachusetts, in 1630 and from there to New York some hundred years later. On my father's side I come from English and Scottish families who also settled the Middle Atlantic colonies before the American Revolution. All these strong-willed, Calvinist, fiercely independent (my grandmother called it *pigheaded*) men and women have been a major influence on me, and on my writing, through the anecdotes, customs, and values that were passed down the generations.

I was born in Ridgewood, New Jersey (in the house described in *Shadow of a Unicorn* and *Ready or Not*), and (with side excursions to Boston, New York, and elsewhere) have lived in the Ridgewood area ever since. I was an only child, but was dragged to many family reunions of my grandparents' generation—that's where I picked up the family stories I used as a basis of my *Keeping Days* series. I was graduated from high school at barely sixteen, later studied acting at the American Theatre Wing and elsewhere, and received a teaching certificate from Montclair College. I wrote my first book (unpublished) when I was eleven and my second (eventually published) when I was sixteen. In between all my other careers I wrote, and ever since *The Keeping Days* was published, that has been my full-time vocation.

I write in a romantic, often gothic style because I know from experience and from theatre that when you draw people into the circle of a rosy glow, they become more open to the thrust of truth. I write about young people facing today's realities without flinching. I write mysteries, detective stories, and suspense stories because they deal with the universal struggle between good and evil—and besides, they're fun! I write about love—in all the different meanings of the word—and about family, and all of *that* word's different meanings. I write a great deal about broken and blended and nonrelated families, because I see so much of that about me, plus I've had them in my own family and know they aren't the end of the world. Above all, I write of the Keeping Days that remain in our memories forever: of the turning points in which we go from innocence to knowledge; of the abstract truths I believe to be unchanging in a changing world. And of facing change without feeling threatened by it. My grandmother used to say, "The world's going to keep turning whether you want it to or not, and you'd better go forward with it or you'll find yourself going backward!"

I still believe ("in spite of everything," as Anne Frank wrote) that mankind has at heart the potential for good as well as evil; that life is no mere accident or dirty joke but has patterns and meaning and purpose. To me, that's realism. And it's why I write.

Bibliography

Books for Young Adults

As Norma Johnston

1963	*The Wishing Star*
1964	*The Wider Heart*
1965	*Ready or Not*
1966	*The Bridge Between*
1973–81	*Keeping Days* (series)
1975	*Of Time and of Seasons*
1975	*Strangers Dark and Gold*
1976	*A Striving After Wind*
1978	*The Swallow's Song*
1978	*If You Love Me, Let Me Go*
1979	*The Crucible Year*
1979	*Pride of Lions*
1982	*The Days of the Dragon's Seed*
1982	*Timewarp Summer*
1983	*Gabriel's Girl*
1986	*Carlisle Chronicles* (series)
1986	*Watcher in the Mist*
1987	*Shadow of a Unicorn*
1988	*Whisper of the Cat*
1988	*The Potter's Wheel*
1988	*Return to Morocco*
1989	*Such Stuff as Dreams Are Made Of*
1989	*The Delphic Choice*
1989	*Summer of the Citadel*
1989	*The Five Magpies*
1990	*The Web of Trust*

As Pamela Dryden

1982	*Mask for My Heart*
1988	*Riding Home*

As Lavinia Harris

1982	*Dreams and Memories*
1984–86	*Computer Detectives* (series)

As Kate Chambers

1983–84	*Diana Winthrop, Detective* (series)

Books for Younger Readers

As Catherine E. Chambers (selected)

1984   *California Gold Rush: Search for Treasure*
1984   *Flatboats on the Ohio: Westward Bound*
1984   *Indian Days: Life in a Frontier Town*
1984   *Wagons West: Off to Oregon*

As Elizabeth Bolton (selected)

1985   *Ghost in the House*
1985   *The Case of the Wacky Cat*
1985   *The Tree House Detective Club*

As Adrian Robert

1985   *The Awful Mess Mystery*
1985   *My Grandma, the Witch*
1985   *The Secret of the Old Barn*

Books for Adults (as Nicole St. John)

1975   *The Medici Ring*
1976   *Wychwood*
1977   *Guinevera's Gift*

Sandra Scoppettone

As far back as I can remember, I wanted to be a writer. During my twenties I wrote three or four adult novels, but none of them was any good. So I switched to writing in the dramatic form for television, theater, and film. I managed to sell one film (never made), write for two soaps, and have several plays produced Off-Off Broadway.

In the early seventies it became clear to me that if I intended to support myself by writing, I would have to try something else. Then a serendipitous thing happened. During the summer of 1973 I was asked to direct a musical using high school students. This was how my first YA novel, *Trying Hard to Hear You*, was born.

Two boys in the cast were gay and the other kids shunned them. Being gay myself, I didn't let the situation get out of hand, as the director in the book does. When the summer was over, I wanted to write about the experience and thought young adult novels might be the right place for the story. I always read a great deal in whatever field I'm going to try, so I read many YA books that fall.

After selling *Trying Hard* I decided to write about another issue, alcoholism, which concerned me, as I am a recovered alcoholic. That book became *The Late Great Me*.

I've been accused of writing hot topics to make money, but it isn't true. The books I've written have been about important issues in my own life or in the lives of people I've known.

Although I've written three adult novels under my own name, I also write mysteries under a pseudonym. At the moment I don't have plans to write another YA book, but you never know.

I live in a loft in an area in New York City called SoHo, with my mate. She is also a writer and we have been together for more than sixteen years. We used to have two dogs and three cats, but only one cat, Gilda, remains. She is orange and white and rules supreme!

Things I dislike: dancing, going to big parties, being on a diet, people who think they are always right, bad reviews, fancy restaurants, any circus.

Things I like: gambling in Atlantic City (in moderation, of course), Ben and Jerry's Coffee Heathbar Crunch and New York Super Fudge Chocolate Chunk, playing with my computer, reading, renting movies to see on our VCR, playing or watching tennis, browsing in used book stores, traveling, getting letters, listening to music.

Oh, yes, I almost forgot . . . I enjoy writing, too!

Bibliography

Books for Young Adults

1974	*Trying Hard to Hear You*
1976	*The Late Great Me*
1978	*Happy Endings Are All Alike*
1982	*Long Time Between Kisses*
1985	*Playing Murder*

Books for Adults

1977	*Some Unknown Person*
1980	*Such Nice People*
1983	*Innocent Bystander*

Ouida Sebestyen

PHOTO: CORBIN SEBESTYEN

ne of my earliest memories is of wandering away from home when I was about two. My mother rushed to tell my father, who was teaching at a little country school nearby. He and his class immediately began to search, followed within minutes by the whole school. I was found happily exploring a distant field of cotton. When I look back, it seems this small adventure foreshadowed some of the main themes of my life and fiction: my sense of being a loved and vital member of the human family, and my joy in nature, new places, solitude, observation—and doing my own thing.

In a way I was lucky to spend my first thirty years in or near the little north Texas town of Vernon, breathing the old dust of Indian battles, cattle drives, oil fields, and melting-pot people. But I was a shy, sickly only child, and wanted the rest of the world. Reading gave it to me.

Smitten, I longed to make the magic that writers made. I began writing with a friend in high school, and during my twenties worked up the courage to start sending stories and novels out to publishers. Three stories actually were accepted, but that blast of encouragement had to carry me through my thirties and forties (and the ego-shrinking receipt of four hundred rejection slips) and into my fifties—when I sold three more. In the meantime I had married and had a son, had divorced, and had formed a three-generation family with my widowed mother. Common sense told me to give up the dream, see to my shattered finances, and concentrate on raising my delightful kid. But impulsively I sent one of my early stories to an editor, asking if she thought it might be worth enlarging to novel length. She said try it, and *Words by Heart* came pouring out.

188

My second book, *Far from Home*, was, in part, a kind of thank-you to the time and place I grew up in. Before I could set *IOU's* in Boulder, Colorado, I had to live there fifteen years, afraid I might not be heeding the rule to "write about what you know." Perhaps there's more of me in this book than in my others, but I secretly believe I'm every character I create.

Writing *On Fire* helped me turn loose of the family responsible for the tragedy in *Words by Heart*. I had really needed to know how their lives went, afterward. *The Girl in the Box* is a mystery, but not a whodunit; the mysteries are the big, universal ones about life and death, evil and good. I wrote it still fascinated—as that long-ago exploring child was—by the world and all its wonders.

Bibliography

1979   *Words by Heart*
1980   *Far from Home*
1982   *IOU's*
1985   *On Fire*
1988   *The Girl in the Box*

Zoa Sherburne

Almost all of the important events in my life have taken place in Seattle, Washington. I was born there, spent most of my school years there, met and married my husband, had my eight children, wrote my first short story, my first poem, and my first novel, all in this lovely, sprawling city on the shores of Puget Sound.

I like to think of myself as a novelist, but the truth is that I had written and sold over three hundred short stories and almost as many poems (I called them verses) before I sat down before my typewriter and started on *Almost April*. My agent, Ann Elmo, had been urging me to try a novel, and the editor of *Seventeen* magazine added her voice, but I was frankly afraid of . . . all those words. I had all the right excuses.

I was happy writing short stories. I could squeeze my writing into odd hours between keeping house, cooking, baking, bowling with my husband, being a den mother again and again and again . . . soooooooo, more to show myself that it wasn't possible than for any other reason, I wrote *Almost April*. I wrote about an obnoxious girl who disliked her grandmother and quarreled loudly with her father and fell in love with an unsavory character. I did all the things you weren't supposed to do in a novel for teenagers and then a scary thing happened. Karen, my viewpoint character, took over. I could feel her at my elbow . . . whispering in my ear, patting my shoulder, nudging me. I wrote and I wrote. I still had a husband (a darling, gentle, encouraging husband), a large house, and three-and-a-half noisy, demanding adorable children. And now I had Karen to cope with.

Karen became Leeanne, who became Eden, who became twelve additional girls as the days and the weeks and the months rolled by.

190

Writing was never work for me. I look back on those years as the happiest, the most fulfilling in my life. I was up early, making breakfasts, packing lunches, finding lost shoes and schoolbooks. I was still banging the typewriter late at night, but in between I had my lovely family and friends who put up with me. In later years I had another bonus . . . grandchildren!

Some of my writing brought me more attention than I deserved. "From Mother With Love," a short story which appeared originally in *Seventeen*, has appeared in sixteen anthologies. "Stranger in the House" was a TV "Movie of the Week" and is still shown from time to time. The title was changed to "Memories Never Die," and it starred Lindsay Wagner.

Across the years, I have lectured and taught, in addition to my writing and my family. I received the Child Study Association Award for my book *Jennifer*. I have traveled back and forth across the country appearing at writers' conferences, book fairs, and conventions.

After my husband's death in 1966, I continued to write with five children still at home, an invalid mother-in-law, and the necessity of keeping a roof over the house. I had little choice. But when I am gone I hope people will remember me as a person who had everything: a wonderful marriage, eight beautiful children (four of each), a strong faith, and (so far) twenty-four grandchildren plus five great-grandchildren. I have enjoyed a successful career for a great many years. I have wonderful friends both in and out of the writing business. I could write a book about the ups and downs, the joys and frustrations, of combining a large active family with a writing career.

AND MAYBE I WILL!

Bibliography

Books for Young Adults

1956	*Almost April*
1957	*The High Wall*
1958	*Princess in Denim*
1959	*Jennifer*
1960	*Evening Star*
1961	*Ballerina on Skates*
1963	*Girl in the Shadows*

Books for Adults

William Sleator

I grew up in University City, Missouri, just outside of St. Louis. I was always writing or composing something musical—and was always fascinated by the grotesque and macabre. One of my first musical compositions was called "Guillotines in the Springtime." When we had to write a story for school about a holiday, I always came up with something like "The Haunted Easter Egg."

When the high school orchestra played one of my compositions at an assembly, everybody thought I was a genius. I did nothing to correct this impression. I went to Harvard, where I was miserable. I prevented myself from going crazy by keeping a voluminous journal, and gave the different volumes titles like *Rats Live on No Evil Star.* (That is a palindrome.)

After college I spent a year in England, studying musical composition and working as a pianist at the Royal Ballet School. In England, I had the experiences that became my first novel, *Blackbriar.* I really did live in an ancient cottage in the middle of the woods that had been a pesthouse for people with smallpox. I was still keeping a journal (and still am), so I remembered all the details. The fact that I had really lived in such a peculiar place gave my first efforts a certain validity. The second editor who saw it, Ann Durell at Dutton, thought there might be something there, and after working with me through several drafts, eventually published it. I have been working happily with her ever since.

I also worked for nine years as rehearsal pianist with the Boston Ballet, touring with them all over Europe and the United States, and composing three ballets that the company performed. It could hardly have been less glamorous, traveling to exotic places like Taormina and seeing nothing but the inside of rehearsal rooms—the pianist, I soon found out, was the only person who had to be at *every* rehearsal. I have lots of material about performing in ancient Roman amphitheaters in the rain, and vicious onstage brawls over boxes of Kleenex. Eventually, the totalitarianism of the ballet company began to annoy me, and I happily quit the job.

Now I write mostly science fiction. What I like about the genre is that you can learn about real scientific phenomena, such as chaos and black holes and strange attractors, and then turn them into stories. I try to write books that are magical and fantastic but at the same time might really be possible. I own a Victorian rowhouse in Boston, where I indulge in occasional binges of heavy cooking. I also do a lot of traveling to Asia.

I consider myself to be one of the most fortunate people in the world to be able to make my living writing books. I just hope I don't run out of ideas. I shouldn't, in a universe that contains such bizarre and contradictory items as the Berkhof Bagel, the Menger sponge, and the human race.

Bibliography

Books for Young Adults

1972	*Blackbriar*
1973	*Run*
1974	*House of Stairs*
1979	*Into the Dream*
1981	*The Green Future of Tycho*
1983	*Fingers*
1984	*Interstellar Pig*
1985	*Singularity*
1986	*The Boy Who Reversed Himself*
1988	*The Duplicate*
1990	*Strange Attractors*

Other Books

1970	*The Angry Moon*, illus. by Blair Lent
1975	*Among the Dolls*, illus. by Trina Schart Hyman
1976	*Take Charge* (with Dr. William H. Redd)
1979	*Once, Said Darlene*, illus. by Steven Kellogg
1981	*That's Silly*, illus. by Lawrence DiFiori

Zilpha Keatley Snyder

I spent my childhood in a fantastical world, full of wild and wonderful adventures.

Actually, I was born and raised in rural southern California in what might have been a rather limited and ordinary environment, if it hadn't been for an accident of birth. In my case the accident was that I seemed to have been born telling stories and playing games.

Storytelling can get you in trouble when you are a kid—even when you're not really a liar but just someone who can't resist making a story really worth telling. My mother used to sigh and say, "Just tell it—don't embroider it."

As a game player I invented exciting scenarios for every part of my daily life. I had games and plays that went with everything. Getting up in the morning, eating breakfast, walking to school, doing chores, going to bed at night—all had their accompanying game. I walked to school as various famous and exciting people— for several months as Queen Nefertiti of ancient Egypt. I carried the trash out to the incinerator as a wartime messenger carrying secret documents through enemy lines. And I did the dishes as a poor frightened slave or mistreated orphan. My games featured magical friends, cruel giants and other monsters, and every sort of strange and wonderful happening.

I also seem to have been born reading, or very nearly. I can't remember a time when books and stories were not a part of my life. I read everything I could get my hands on, and of course the characters and events in books played important parts in my exciting daily scenarios. As I got older my fascination with books and stories inspired a desire to write, to tell my stories and scenarios in writing.

But eventually I had to grow up, or at least pretend to. I went to college, got married, had children of my own, and taught school for several years. But the writing dream remained, and it was when I decided to try something for the age level that I had been teaching that I became a professional storyteller. My first book was published in 1964, and I am now working on my twenty-fifth. All of my books are fiction—for me writing anything else is simply a chore—and many of my stories have a touch of the fantastical.

Nowadays I get letters from readers all over the country, wonderful letters full of insightful comments and questions. One of the most common questions is "Where do you get your ideas?"

My answer to that favorite question is simply this: getting ideas is not a matter of having interesting or unusual sources. Everyone has good source material. Getting ideas is simply a habit, one that all young children have to some extent. It is the habit of taking bits and pieces of reality and *building* on them for your own entertainment.

So if you want to write, hang on to the magical stone that you found in your backyard, the dog that talks to you when no one else is around, even the monsters that are hiding under your bed—and hang on to your own natural-born ability to build on reality.

Bibliography

Books for Young Adults

1964   *Season of Ponies*
1965   *The Velvet Room*
1966   *Black and Blue Magic*
1967   *The Egypt Game*
1968   *Eyes in the Fishbowl*
1970   *The Changeling*
1971   *The Headless Child*
1972   *The Witches of Worm*
1974   *The Truth about Stone Hollow*
1975   *Below the Root*
1976   *And All Between*
1977   *Until the Celebration*
1979   *The Famous Stanley Kidnapping Case*
1981   *A Fabulous Creature*
1983   *The Birds of Summer*

1984	*Blair's Nightmare*
1987	*And Condors Danced*
1988	*Squeek Saves the Day and Other Tooley Tales*
1989	*Janie's Private Eyes*

Books for Younger Readers

1973	*The Princess and the Giants*
1982	*Come On, Patsy*
1985	*The Changing Maze*

Other Books

| 1969 | *Today Is Saturday* (poetry) |
| 1978 | *Heirs of Darkness* (adult novel) |

Jerry Spinelli

I was born in Norristown, Pennsylvania, in 1941. For most of my kid years, we lived in a brick rowhouse in the West End.

I did the usual kid stuff: rode my bike, played chew-the-peg, flipped baseball cards, skimmed flat stones across Stony Creek, cracked twin popsicles, caught poison ivy, wondered about girls, thought stuff that I would never say out loud.

When I was sixteen, my high school football team won a big game. That night I wrote a poem about it. The poem was published in the local newspaper, and right about then I stopped wanting to become a major league shortstop and started wanting to become a writer.

But first I became a grown-up. And I thought, as most grown-ups do: okay, now on to the important stuff.

So I tried writing grown-up novels about important stuff. Nobody wanted them.

In my thirties I married another writer, known to young readers as Eileen Spinelli. Not only did she bring a wagonload of published poems and stories to the marriage, she brought a half-dozen kids. Instant fatherhood.

One night one of our angels snuck into the refrigerator and swiped the fried chicken that I was saving for lunch the next day. When I discovered the chicken was gone, I did what I had done after the big football victory: I wrote about it.

I didn't know it at the time, but I had begun to write my first published novel, *Space Station Seventh Grade*. By the time it was finished, hardly anything in it had to do with my grown-up, "important" years. It was all from the West End days.

And I began to see that in my own memories and in the kids around me, I had all the material I needed for a schoolbagful of books. I saw that each kid is a population unto him- or herself, and that a child's bedroom is as much a window to the universe as an orbiting telescope or a philosopher's study.

I saw that each of us, in our kidhoods, was a Huckleberry Finn, drifting on a current that seemed tortuously slow at times, poling for the shore to check out every slightest glimmer in the trees . . . the taste of brussels sprouts . . . your first forward roll . . . cruising a mall without a parent . . . overnighting it . . . making your own grilled cheese sandwich . . . the weird way you felt when Sally Duffy scrunched next to you in the mob coming out of the movie . . . the thousand landfalls of our adolescence. And the current flows faster and faster, adulthood's delta looms, and one day we look to get our bearings and find that we are out to sea.

And now we know what we did not know then: what an adventure it was!

Bibliography

1982   *Space Station Seventh Grade*
1984   *Who Put That Hair in My Toothbrush?*
1985   *Night of the Whale*
1986   *Jason and Marceline*
1988   *Dump Days*

Mary Stolz

PHOTO: © 1984 VALRIE MASSEY

To write an autobiographical sketch in 450 to 500 words after living close to threescore and ten is a daunting proposition. I've led a pretty bookish life, and though in the past my husband and I traveled a lot, most of the results of that is in my books. However, to do my best:

Born: Boston, 1920.

One sister, Eileen, younger. We grew up with our dear first cousin, Peg. Our mothers were twins. Peg died on my birthday in 1968, just before Martin Luther King, Jr., was assassinated. Not a day has passed that I've not thought of her and missed her, but I do not wish her back to the world as it is now. Often I think of what it was like when we grew up in New York City long ago, during what is now referred to as the Great Depression. We were poor then, but we had books, went to concerts and plays—a couple of dollars a seat, or free in museums and parks. In summer we went to the beautiful beaches of Long Island and New Jersey to bathe in clean waters. We traveled the subways without fear. We did not lock our doors. It seems to me that life in this country, on this planet, is considerably more depressing now than it was during the Depression. Peg was a life-lover of sparkling enthusiasm, even relishing the jolts, if they weren't brutal. By dying when she did, she missed much she'd have wanted to experience. She did not see her sons and daughter grow up to be delightful, decent adults. She never knew her grandchildren. She missed a number of wonderful new books, as well as the greater joy of rereading old ones. Missed some glorious ballet, which she loved, and good baseball, which she didn't care for, but nevertheless there's been some good baseball and she missed it. She lost the continued company of Eileen and me, which she valued. *But.* She did not live to see the entire world in the talons of terrorists for whom the murder of innocents is something to be cackled over. She will not know that an irreversible process of filth and pollution is destroying this planet—its land, its waters. She cares not that we are steadily shredding the ozone layer, which cannot be mended like a tapestry or a pair of socks. It is nothing to Peg that we are smothering in garbage and creating worldwide droughts through a savage policy of deforestation. She did not live to face the shock of our electing, *and* reelecting, Ronald Reagan. We will be paying the price of that presidency well into the next century, should the earth survive its other menaces that long. In only one way are these times better than the times in which I grew up, with Eileen and Peg for company. That is the improved lot of black people in America. By no means do I imply that the situation is good . . . only better than when Ralph Ellison wrote *Invisible Man* and told the stark, unspeakable, unspoken—until he wrote it—truth. I think even Ralph Ellison would agree that some alleviation has been brought about for these citizens of our country. When Peg and Eileen and I grew up, we were unaware of the suffering of black people, because they *were* invisible. So—one step forward.

An autobiography is supposed to tell where you've been, what you've done, and what you've thought in your life. To my surprise, I think I've accomplished that in the required wordspan.

Bibliography (selected)

1950	*To Tell Your Love*
1951	*The Sea Gulls Woke Me*
1953	*Truth or Consequences*
1954	*Pray Love, Remember*
1956	*Hospital Zone*
1958	*Second Nature*
1962	*Fredou*
1962	*Pigeon Flight*
1963	*The Bully of Barkham Street*
1964	*The Mystery of the Woods*
1966	*Maximillian's World*
1969	*Dragons of the Queen*
1971	*By the Highway Home*
1972	*Leap Before You Look*
1974	*The Edge of Next Year*
1974	*Cat in the Mirror*

Todd Strasser

PHOTO: PAM OBER

The most difficult aspects of being a teenager, for me, had to do with judgment and making choices. I grew up in suburban Long Island, and in the 1960s we rebelled against The Establishment. The Establishment said the war in Vietnam was good and the counterculture (long hair, rock music, drugs) was bad, and in retrospect they were mostly wrong on the first count and sometimes right (drugs) on the second. At the time, they appeared to be dead wrong on both counts and I was about as countercultural as they came, and caused my parents all sorts of grief.

When I look back on my adolescence I'm thankful that I survived. I have small children of my own now, and I already wonder how I'll handle their teenage years. Almost all my books, starting with *Angel Dust Blues* and *Friends Till the End,* and going through *A Very Touchy Subject* and *The Accident,* concern teens dealing with the kinds of choices I faced. Sometimes I think I write YA books because I'm still trying to resolve the conflicts of my own youth. When I say that I hope that each of my books shows an example of a young adult who learns good judgment, I sometimes want to add, "because I wish I'd had it when I was a teen."

Even in the midst of conflict and turmoil, we could usually share a laugh. I think this came from my grandfather, who profited from every loss by turning it into a humorous anecdote. For instance, he used to tell the story of when I was three and he took me clamming near his summer home in Bayville. Leaving me in the boat, he hopped into the shoulder-deep water and began digging the clams with a rake and throwing them into a bushel basket in the boat. As fast as he threw clams in, I dropped them back over the side. He dug in the same spot for almost an hour, amazed at how plentiful the clams were. Of course, when he climbed back into the boat and found an empty basket, he realized what had happened.

I guess it's no surprise that my characters sometimes turn to humor in a tough moment. When I think of Tony facing a new school in *The Complete Computer Popularity Program*, and Scott facing new hormones in *A Very Touchy Subject*, I know my grandfather would be proud.

Sports has been another significant influence in my life. These days I play tennis, ski, and fish. Through high school I tried almost all the competitive sports. David in *Friends Till the End* is a soccer player and Matt in *The Accident* is a swimmer. I've always found physical activity a necessary outlet, as do the characters in my books. Even Gary, the rock musician in my trilogy, *Rock 'N' Roll Nights, Turn It Up!* and *Wildlife,* goes out and shoots baskets between concerts.

In recent years I've done a lot of traveling around the country, speaking at schools and conferences about writing and YA books. This too has had an influence on my writing. My first books were almost always set in familiar environs such as New York and its suburbs, but my more recent works take place in Colorado (*The Accident*), Florida (*Beyond the Reef*—about diving for sunken treasure), and Alaska.

The more I write, the harder it seems to get, probably because my standards for myself have grown more exacting over the years. Still, I love getting up in the morning, making a mug of tea, and sitting down at the word processor. There is nothing I'd rather do.

When I'm not on the road speaking at a school or conference, I live in New York City with my wife and two children.

Bibliography

1979	*Angel Dust Blues*
1981	*Friends Till the End*
1981	*The Wave* (novelization)
1982	*Rock 'N' Roll Nights*
1983	*Workin' for Peanuts*
1984	*Turn It Up!*
1984	*The Complete Computer Popularity Program*
1985	*A Very Touchy Subject*
1986	*Ferris Bueller's Day Off* (novelization)

Rosemary Sutcliff

 **I** was born only a few years after the end of the First World War, and during my first nine years my mother and I trailed round after my father, who was a naval officer: Malta when I was two, Sheerness Dockyard when I was five, two years lodgings on the bleak North Kent coast while my father was in South Africa, Chatham Dockyard. . . .

Partly as a result of all this globe-trotting, partly because I contracted juvenile arthritis when I was three, I never went to school during that time, but my mother, in her own splendidly unorthodox fashion, taught me at home, chiefly by reading to me. King Arthur and Robin Hood, myths and legends of the classical world, *The Wind in the Willows, The Tailor of Gloucester, Treasure Island, Nicholas Nickleby, Kim, Puck of Pook's Hill,* and *Little Women,* all at more or less the same time. The result was that at the age of nine I was happily at home with a rich and somewhat indigestible stirabout of literature, but was not yet able to read to myself. Why, after all, read to yourself when you can get somebody else to read to you?

When I was ten, my father retired from the navy and we went to live near his boyhood home in Devon; and I, having at last learned to read, went to Proper School for the first time. I stuck it for four years, during which I learned virtually nothing; and at the end of that time my parents, with wisdom beyond their years, allowed me to leave, which you could do at fourteen in those days, and go to art school.

I finished my art student years just as World War II broke out. I had taken the three-year general art course and done quite well, but when decision time came, my tutors and parents told me that I would never be able to handle a big canvas and had better take up miniature painting. I did not think at the time to point out that the Mona Lisa is only around thirteen inches square. I took up miniature painting.

I was reasonably good at it, and several works of mine were hung at the Royal Academy, but I always felt cramped by the smallness of the work, and finally, chiefly as a means of gaining wing-spreading space, I started writing, gradually giving up painting altogether as the books took over. My first book, *The Queen Elizabeth Story*, was published in 1950.

Given the kind of books my mother had filled me with in my earliest years, it is not surprising that historical novels seemed to me the natural and obvious books to write; and with my very special love for Rudyard Kipling's three wonderful Romano British stories in *Puck of Pook's Hill*, it is not surprising that once my first tentative efforts were over, I turned to Roman and Dark Age Britain for many of my stories. I am writing another of them at the moment, with the working title of *The Shining Company*.

Why I should write almost entirely for children and young adults, I have not the least idea; it just happens that way, by no conscious choice of mine.

Bibliography

Books for Young Adults

1954	*The Eagle of the Ninth*
1955	*Outcast*
1956	*The Shield Ring*
1957	*The Silver Branch*
1958	*Warrior Scarlet*
1959	*The Lantern Bearers*
1960	*Houses and History*
1960	*Knight's Fee*
1960	*Rudyard Kipling*
1961	*Beowulf*
1961	*Dawn Wind*
1963	*The Hound of Ulster*
1965	*Heroes and History*
1965	*The Mark of the Horse Lord*
1967	*The Chief's Daughter*

1967	*The High Deeds of Finn Mac Cool*
1968	*A Circlet of Oak Leaves*
1971	*Tristan and Iseult*
1971	*Truce of the Games*
1973	*The Capricorn Bracelet*
1974	*The Changeling*
1976	*Blood Feud*
1977	*Sun Horse, Moon Horse*
1977	*Shifting Sands*
1978	*Song for a Dark Queen*
1979	*The Light Beyond the Forest*
1980	*Frontier Wolf*
1980	*Three Legions*
1981	*Eagle's Egg*
1981	*The Road to Camlann*
1982	*Blue Remembered Hills*
1983	*Bonnie Dundee*
1987	*A Little Dog Like You*

Books for Younger Readers

1950	*The Chronicles of Robin Hood*
1950	*The Queen Elizabeth Story*
1951	*The Armourer's House*
1952	*Brother Dusty-Feet*
1953	*Simon*
1965	*A Saxon Settler*
1970	*The Witch's Brat*
1985	*Flame Coloured Taffeta*
1986	*The Roundabout Horse*

Books for Adults

1956	*Lady in Waiting*
1959	*The Rider of the White Horse*
1963	*Sword at Sunset*
1969	*The Flowers of Adonis*
1987	*Blood and Sand*

Joyce Carol Thomas

I was reluctant to leave Ponca City, Oklahoma, where I was born. As we boarded the train to California in 1948, I celebrated my tenth birthday, enjoying the traveling adventure but longing to be back in the place I knew. When I look at my books, I suddenly realize that I have never really left Oklahoma. *Marked by Fire* is set in Ponca City, and so are *Bright Shadow* and *The Golden Pasture.* Going to a new place held its own excitement, too, and the California landscape became the setting of *Water Girl* and *Journey.*

A sense of place, as you can see, is very important to me. But what is most important is my desire to tell a good story. I work to create characters from the depths of my imagination. I want them to be so real that they come again and again to my readers' attention and linger long after the book is closed. I was lucky enough to hear such stories. From my mother and my aunts and the women of Ponca City I heard ghost stories of a woman looking for her children in the graveyard, of men with heads and no bodies floating in the weed fields, stories that made the hair stand up on the back of my neck. Because I was born before television, we had to entertain ourselves. And so when I write, I like to write as though my readers are without television, radio, movies, or anything else. I hope to involve them so thoroughly in the love story of *Bright Shadow* that they become Abyssinia or Carl Lee or any of the other characters. I want them to care about what happens to my people.

Also, I cannot afford to bore myself when I write, so I like to do something different in each book. Go in another direction. Even create a horror story, as I did in *Journey.*

I began my writing career as a poet with training in Latin, Spanish, and French. I was already a poet because I began to compose poetry before I was six years old. Also, after receiving my master's degree from Stanford University, I taught junior high school students. Since then I have taught university-level students and find that teaching is a wonderful asset to my writing career. I understand a lot of what today's young people think because of my years of teaching.

I care a great deal about the craft of fiction and I am extremely disciplined. I write about six hours a day, sometimes more if my characters are excited about something.

Music holds either a major or a minor place in my stories. In high school I played first chair, second violin. And while I could not sing, I always wanted to. My characters can do some of the things I wanted to do. Abyssinia Jackson, for instance, is a dynamite vocalist. Carl Lee Jefferson plays a fantastic cello.

My advice to young people who want to write is to read everything that fascinates you. And to spin a tale every now and then, and to let your imagination run amuck. You can always edit anything too outrageous out of what you've written. Then again, somebody just might want to read something outrageous. I would.

Bibliography

Books for Young Adults

1982   *Marked by Fire*
1983   *Bright Shadow*
1986   *Water Girl*
1986   *The Golden Pasture*
1988   *Journey*

Books of Poetry

1973   *Bittersweet*
1974   *Crystal Breezes*
1974   *Blessing*
1981   *Black Child*
1982   *Inside the Rainbow*

Plays

Julian F. Thompson

I was born the son of poor but honest woodcutters in New York City. The first three and the last four words of that are true. My father wrote a play called *The Warrior's Husband,* in which Katharine Hepburn had her first starring Broadway role; that's entirely true, although in fact my father was a businessman, and wrote just as a hobby. Instead of reading stories to my sister and myself at night, he used to tuck us in and say, "Now tell *yourself* a story." And we did. I think I thought that everybody did. My father was a clever man, who loved his children well.

In school, there were two kinds of writing that we had to do. One was "on an assigned topic," and the other was called "free composition." Most kids liked the first kind best, but I preferred the second. In free composition, I could take the stories that I'd told myself and get, in one sense, *paid* for them. That idea appealed to me, a lot.

In college, I remember writing quite a major paper on Plato in the style of Damon Runyon. In those days, a lot of students still turned in papers written in longhand, and my professor took thirty points off my grade because, he said, I had a "sentence error" in the paper, and because I hadn't dotted any of my i's. I was furious; I was sure I hadn't made a sentence error and I proved that to him. He gave me ten points back. I still was furious, of course. Next time, I dotted all my i's with little circles. Yes, I was a sophomore at the time.

Most college "men" who've reached the dignity of twenty don't hang out with teenagers a lot, other than the ones whose names are Penny, Annabel, and Candy, who they know will be impressed by all their worldly ways. Not me. In addition to the

Pennys, Annabels, and Candys, I spent more time with various assorted teens in the next twenty-five years than with any other age group. I had good friends that age who were in the state reformatory, and in summer camps, a boarding school, and finally in another school we started up from scratch. In that one, I ran a writing workshop for seven years, and in it did the same assignments that the other students did, each day. I think I found my writing "voice" while doing that. When I finally left the world of school, I began to write about the people I had known, trying to bring their attitudes, concerns, and caring to the printed page.

I think we human beings face a lot of problems that are deadly serious. I also think we're perfectly ridiculous, at times. My books reflect those two opinions, as well as my concerns about the way some people try to bring up kids, and teach them. I think a future generation can produce a cleaner, more humane, more democratic world than this one. I always hope that it'll be the next one.

Bibliography

1983   *The Grounding of Group Six*
1983   *Facing It*
1984   *A Question of Survival*
1985   *Discontinued*
1986   *A Band of Angels*
1987   *Simon Pure*
1988   *The Taking of Mariasburg*
1989   *Goofbang Value Daze*

John Rowe Townsend

I was born in an old and ordinary part of Leeds, a big industrial city in the north of England. In those days Leeds had acres and acres of humble rowhouses, punctuated with little alleyways and corner shops. They were my first background, and deep inside me I shall always be a boy from the back streets of Leeds.

I went straight from high school to work, but was rescued educationally by World War II, in which I served with the R.A.F. in the Middle East and Italy. I came back with my mind considerably broadened and the prospect of a veteran's grant, and, improbably, managed to talk my way into Cambridge University to study English literature.

At Cambridge I edited the student newspaper, which helped me to get a job after graduation with the *Manchester Guardian*. I was a subeditor, then picture editor, then for some years editor of the weekly international edition. But the time comes when one wants to do something longer-lasting than journalism. I'd reviewed children's fiction and found much of it disappointingly bland and hygienic. It occurred to me that the city streets I knew might provide a setting for a children's book with more flavor. The result was *Gumble's Yard* (in America, *Trouble in the Jungle*), which was about a family of poor children and was set in a background similar to the one I grew up in.

Gumble's Yard was a success (it is still in print in the U.K. after twenty-seven years), and other books followed. My earnings were modest at first, but gradually rose to more than my newspaper salary, and it seemed time to go it alone. I was married by now, with three children, and of course I consulted my wife. "If that's what you want to do," she told me, "do it." So I took the plunge, became a professional writer, and have survived as one for twenty years. It hasn't made me rich, but it's been a good life.

I particularly enjoy writing for young adults, and agree with a British colleague, John Gordon, who described adolescence as "border country, a passionate place in which to work." I am fascinated by people grappling with circumstances at the very limits of their abilities and endurance. I like to explore moral problems, but I don't like to lay down the law about them. Books are for asking questions, not for answering them.

As for settings, I like all places that are in some sense at the end of the world. I love islands, because islands have so much adventure built into them and because a lot of action and emotion can be concentrated in a small space. I enjoy writing comedy, as in *Kate and the Revolution*. Above all, I'm endlessly interested in the ways in which people interact with each other. Human relationships, the human heart, the human predicament—I believe that in the end these are what all worthwhile fiction is about.

My job, as I see it, is to write the best book I can, whatever it may be. One thing I am sure of is that a book for young readers must be a good book, period.

Bibliography

Books for Young Adults

1963	*Hell's Edge*
1969	*The Intruder*
1970	*Goodnight, Prof, Love* (in U.S., *Goodnight, Prof, Dear*)
1972	*The Summer People*
1975	*Noah's Castle*
1977	*The Xanadu Manuscript* (in U.S., *The Visitors*)
1980	*King Creature, Come* (in U.S., *The Creatures*)
1981	*The Islanders*
1982	*A Foreign Affair* (in U.S., *Kate and the Revolution*)
1984	*Cloudy-Bright*
1987	*Downstream*
1989	*The Golden Journey* (in U.S., *The Fortunate Isles*)

Books for Children

1961	*Gumble's Yard* (in U.S., *Trouble in the Jungle*)
1965	*Widdershins Crescent* (in U.S., *Goodbye to the Jungle*)

1968	*Pirate's Island*
1976	*Top of the World*
1983	*Dan Alone*
1985	*Tom Tiddler's Ground*
1986	*The Persuading Stick*
1987	*Rob's Place*

Books for Adults

1965	*Written for Children: An Outline of English-language Children's Literature*
1971	*A Sense of Story: Essays on Contemporary Writers for Children* (revised edition published 1979 as *A Sounding of Storytellers: New and Revised Essays on Contemporary Writers for Children*)
1971	*Modern Poetry: A selection by John Rowe Townsend* (editor)

Cynthia Voigt

A friend recently re-marked to me, "You are so *nor*-mal." She said it in frustration, meaning so disappointingly nor-mal, so boringly normal; she said it in protest, meaning that she didn't think I was normal at all. My mother said about the same thing, although she said it laugh-ing—at me and at herself—as she was trying to write a biographical sketch of me: "You have had," she told me, "a very dull life."

I'm not about to quarrel with either of them, although I've found my life interesting to live. The facts bear them out: a secure childhood, spent among siblings and friends and books, in a world run by adults who enjoyed taking their responsibilities seriously; that New England women's education, designed to foster indepen-dence of mind and recognizing that willfulness and rebellion af-firmed rather than undermined its purposes; an employment that, while the world might find it unhonorable and unenviable, is deeply satisfying to the whole person; a failed marriage from which I emerged with a continued friendship and a wonderful child; a more successful marital endeavor with a good friend and good thinker, which has given me another terrific kid. And I get to write books.

It is that last entry that seems to elevate my life from the dull and normal range. But think about it. Writing books, the actual work of it, can qualify as the least exciting of occupations; *to write*, is among the least active of action verbs, just above *to think*. To do it, you sit down, stay still. From the outside, if, say, a movie camera were focused on the writer at work, the words *boring* and *dull* would spring to mind. This is, however, only true from the outside. Inside, secretly, invisibly, the right writing of a paragraph or a good telling of a story tastes like an adventure as exciting as any I've heard about, taken part in, or imagined. So that the facade of writing, or maybe it's the secretive quality of it, seems to me a metaphor for my life. I begin to wonder about the lives of all the people I see, all the so-called normal people. I begin to suspect that it is normal to be, like an iceberg, more than you seem to be, to be not only what you seem to be.

When I graduated from college, there were two things I knew for sure and certain about myself. I knew I wanted to be a writer. I knew I did not want to be a teacher. Imagine my surprise, then, to find that, necessity having driven me into a classroom, I not only loved teaching but was also good at it. Now imagine my frustration when for years and years and years, nothing I wrote interested anybody I submitted the work to; and then my excitement when at last I sold a manuscript. As things have turned out, I have to know that I was both one hundred percent right about myself, and one hundred percent wrong.

Bibliography

1981   *Homecoming*
1982   *Tell Me If the Lovers Are Losers*
1982   *Dicey's Song*
1983   *The Callender Papers*
1983   *A Solitary Blue*
1984   *Building Blocks*
1985   *The Runner*
1985   *Jackaroo*
1986   *Izzy, Willy-Nilly*
1986   *Stories About Rosie*
1986   *Come a Stranger*
1987   *Sons from Afar*
1988   *Tree by Leaf*
1989   *Seventeen Against the Dealer*

Jill Paton Walsh

I was born in an everyday suburb of London in 1937, and brought up there when not moved for safety to Cornwall; there was a war going on. Hitler made me a writer; for long tracts of my childhood in and out of air-raid shelters there was nothing to do but read; and the only available books in my surroundings were bound sets of Victorian classics. Literature seemed more real to me than life, and much more interesting. By and by I won a scholarship to study English at Oxford. Oxford made me a children's writer; who could sniff at children's books under the twin looming presences of Professors Lewis and Tolkien? Or who, struggling with Beowulf, and Gawain, and Chaucer could think there was anything wrong with dragons, magic, and strong story lines? So, I read adult books as a child, and as an adult wrote children's books.

I have happily spent large tracts of life wrestling with the fascinating technical demands of writing books which are fully adult while being fully accessible to children. A writer's life is not superficially very interesting—all the important events in it are inner events. I have raised three children, travelled a little, talked to friends, and spent many hours sitting at a sequence of machines—first a battered manual typewriter, then an electric one with coloured ribbons, then a primitive word processor, now a sophisticated one. There is nothing to see about this process, and nothing to tell about it except the books that emerge.

My secret life, though, is huge fun. I pursue anything I get interested in—history, romantic places, interesting people, crazy ideas, foreign languages—and often find a book to write waiting in my latest "craze." I have been to many places—down a coal mine,

219

round a cotton mill, just up the road to look at the fen . . . no two days the same.

These days I live and work in Cambridge, England, although I often visit the United States, and I sometimes write adult novels between children's books. I am learning modern Greek—why? well, why not?—and am just off to Egypt to look at a sphinx.

Like most other writers I don't get rich in money, only in everything else.

Bibliography

Books for Children and Young Adults

1966   Hengest's Tale
1967   The Dolphin Crossing
1969   Wordhoard (with Kevin Crossley Holland)
1970   Fireweed
1972   Farewell, Great King
1972   Goldengrove
1973   Toolmaker
1973   The Dawnstone
1974   The Emperor's Winding Sheet
1975   The Butty Boy
1975   The Island Sunrise: Prehistoric Britain
1976   Unleaving
1979   A Chance Child
1981   The Green Book (reissued as Shine)
1984   A Parcel of Patterns
1985   Gaffer Samson's Luck
1986   Five Tides
1987   Torch

Series

1977–78   Children of the Fox (Crossing to Salamis, The Walls of Athens, Persian Gold)

Picture Books

1982   *Babylon,* illus. by Jenny Northway
1984   *Lost and Found,* illus. by Mary Rayner

Books for Adults

1986   *Lapsing*
1989   *A School for Lovers*

Laurence Yep

PHOTO: K. YEP

I was born in 1948 in San Francisco, where I lived in a black ghetto but commuted every day to a school in Chinatown. As a result, I was always something of an outsider. In my neighborhood, I could serve as the all-purpose Asian in war games—being cast either as the Japanese or the Korean Communist who got killed depending on what war we were fighting.

Even in Chinatown, I felt like an outsider. Since I went to a Catholic school, my Chinese-American friends would tell jokes in Chinese so that the nuns would not understand. However, since I couldn't speak Chinese, neither did I.

When I was a child, there weren't any books about Chinese-American children; but when I went to the library, I could never get interested in books about Homer Price or other such children. Every child had a bicycle and no one seemed to worry about locking their front doors. As a result, these and other such details seemed like fantasy to me.

Ironically, what seemed "truer" to me were science fiction and fantasy because in those books children were taken to other lands and other worlds where they had to learn strange customs and languages—and that was something I did every time I got on and off the bus.

Actually, I never intended to be a writer but a chemist. In high school, the chemistry teacher let me work on different sorts of explosives so that I was more inclined toward the sciences. But my English teacher told me that if I wanted an A in his course, I would have to get something accepted by a national magazine. He later retracted that threat, but I had gotten bitten by the submission bug so I kept on sending in stories.

When I was eighteen, I finally sold my first story to a science-fiction magazine for a penny a word—which is the rate Dickens used to get (but pennies went further in his day).

From the very beginning, I think I was dealing with that childhood feeling of being an outsider. That first published story was about a nonhuman told from his viewpoint in the first person; and all the rest of my stories have dealt with being an outsider, from science fiction like *Sweetwater* and *Monster Makers, Inc.* or my fantasy books, like *Dragon of the Lost Sea* and *Dragon Steel*, to the books about Mark Twain, *The Mark Twain Murders* and *The Tom Sawyer Fires*. Even my contemporary books, *Kind Hearts and Gentle Monsters* and *Liar, Liar,* are about teenagers who place themselves outside of society.

In fact, I still sketch out a science-fiction story before I begin a book about Chinese-American history. But my Chinese-American books are a way of stepping into the shoes of members of my family: my father in *Dragonwings*, my mother in *Child of the Owl*, my grandmother in *Serpent's Children* and *Mountain Light,* and myself in *Sea Glass*.

Any writer is something of an outsider. Only the discontented have reason to daydream, and perhaps that makes us professional daydreamers who get paid to write down their dreams.

Bibliography

Books for Young Adults

1973	*Sweetwater*
1975	*Dragonwings*
1977	*Child of the Owl*
1979	*Sea Glass*
1981	*Kind Hearts and Gentle Monsters*
1981	*The Mark Twain Murders*
1983	*Liar, Liar*
1983	*Dragon of the Lost Sea*
1984	*Serpent's Children*
1984	*The Tom Sawyer Fires*
1985	*Dragon Steel*
1985	*Mountain Light*
1986	*Monster Makers*
1989	*The Rainbow People*

Other Books

1977   *Seademons*
1985   *Shadow Lord*
1987   *Curse of the Squirrel*

Plays

1987   *Pay the Chinaman*
1987   *Fairy Bones*

Software

1985   *Alice in Wonderland*
1986   *Jungle Book*

Jane Yolen

PHOTO: DAVID STEMPLE

I come from a family of storytellers. My great-grandfather told stories in the inn that he owned in a little Russian village. My mother and father and all my aunts and uncles were wonderful spinners of tales. That means, of course, that I can't really trust the history of our family as told by my relatives. They are better storytellers than historians. My brother, who is a newspaperman in Brazil, is the most honest of us all. His stories, at least, make a pretense at accuracy.

I was born in New York City, but we moved to the country when I was thirteen, so my stories reflect both the city life (*The Wizard of Washington Square*) and the country (*The Transfigured Hart*). Growing up Jewish in New York City gave me an identification with my heritage, but once we moved to the country, there were hardly any Jewish students in my high school in Westport, Connecticut. I became so assimilated that it took me years and years until I finally wrote a story about that particular background. *The Devil's Arithmetic*, my ninety-second book to be published, finally dealt in depth with the feelings I had had when I discovered that not everyone in the world was a Jew.

What I had loved from early on was the magic of fairy tales. As a child I had read all the fairy tales in Andrew Lang's color fairy books—*The Red Fairy Book, The Green Fairy Book,* etc. And in high school and college I had been a folksinger. So the folk and traditional stories and songs were a part of my everyday respirations. I wrote reams of poetry, publishing some in my high school literary magazine and my college literary magazine and, when I was a junior at Smith College, in a small national literary magazine. So it should not be surprising that when I discovered I could write fiction (I had worked on newspapers and thought I was a nonfiction writer and a poet), I began to write fairy tales, that wonderful combination of the poetic muse and the newspaper questioner ("What if . . ."). Such stories began to tumble out of me: *The Emperor and the Kite, Greyling, The Girl Who Cried Flowers, Dream Weaver, Neptune Rising.* It is still my favorite form.

After school I was an editor for five years—three of them as a children's book editor—and then my husband David Stemple and I decided to camp across Europe and the Mid-East. We came back when I was almost eight months pregnant, settled in Massachusetts, where he got a job at the University of Massachusetts, and raised three children. I wrote all the time. I wrote when we were camping, when we worked in a kibbutz in Israel, when we slept in an olive grove in Greece, when we snorkled in the Red Sea, when we joined grape pickers in France for the harvest, when each of my children napped. Writing down my stories has been both work and recreation for me. Quite simply, I found I loved storytelling.

Bits and pieces of my life cross into my fiction. The girl Olivia found in the olive tree in *The Girl Who Cried Flowers* came in part from that camping trip; a scene in *The Stone Silenus* where Melissa nearly drowns comes from the time I fell out of a raft when we were white-water rafting on the Colorado River; Jakkin in *Dragon's Blood* looks a lot and sounds a lot like my son Adam; Melissa in *Silenus* and Sarah in *The Gift of Sarah Barker* are definitely my daughter Heidi; Jeremy in *No Bath Tonight* is my son Jason; the father and daughter in *Owl Moon* are Heidi and my husband David, and so on. But the emotions in most of my books—are mine. So it is with all writers. We write using our own hearts, our own minds, our own bodies and blood. We know it best of all, even the bad parts.

Bibliography

Books for Young Adults

1981	*The Gift of Sarah Barker*
1982	*Neptune Rising*
1983	*Tales of Wonder*
1983	*Dragon's Blood*
1984	*Heart's Blood*
1984	*The Stone Silenus*
1985	*Dragonfield and Other Stories*

1985	*Cards of Grief*
1986	*Merlin's Booke*
1987	*A Sending of Dragons*
1988	*The Devil's Arithmetic*
1988	*Sister Light, Sister Dark*
1988	*Werewolves*
1989	*White Jenna*
1989	*Things That Go Bump in the Night*

Books for Middle Grade Readers

1963	*Pirates in Petticoats*
1969	*The Wizard of Washington Square*
1974	*The Girl Who Cried Flowers*
1974	*The Magic Three of Solatia*
1975	*The Transfigured Hart*
1978	*The Mermaid's Three Wisdoms*
1979	*Dream Weaver*
1981	*The Boy Who Spoke Chimp*
1984	*Children of the Wolf*
1986	*Spaceships and Spells*
1987	*Dragons and Dreams*

Books for Young Children

1967	*The Emperor and the Kite*
1968	*Greyling*
1978	*No Bath Tonight*
1987	*Owl Moon*

Paul Zindel

All anyone would want to know about me is in my novel *The Amazing and Death-Defying Diary of Eugene Dingman.* I am Eugene. In fact, my full name is Paul Eugene Zindel, and the only big difference between my real life and Eugene Dingman's life is that I had him live in Bayonne, New Jersey, and I grew up in Staten Island, New York. Such are the tricks we fiction writers enjoy: we disguise the fact that we're usually, in one way or another, writing about our own lives and experiences. In my book *A Begonia for Miss Applebaum,* I call myself Henry Ledniz, and only the swiftest of my readers will be able to see through the secret of *Ledniz.*

I think my books are successful because I have a tremendous empathy for young adults. A great part of me inside is still very young, and adolescence is a time for problem-solving—for dealing with the awesome questions of self-identity, responsibility, authority, sex, love, God, and death. These are truthfully life-long questions, but kids especially love to talk about The Great Questions. Once upon a time I was a science teacher, and one of my classes wanted to write all the ways it could think of to die in this world. On the blackboard they wrote down things like fire, diphtheria, python constrictions, plane crashes, scurvy, elephantiasis, decapitation. . . . One kid even remembered a little girl at Coney Island being run down by a miniature locomotive and getting a miniature death. By the end of the period, they had the blackboards covered, crammed full of ways to die!

I think action and suspense are the most important elements in all of writing for young people. I learned that when I was a student at Port Richmond High School and my English teacher tried to commit suicide. Her name was Miss Burger. Miss Burger was the only one in the school who didn't think I was a misfit. And she was the only high school teacher I had ever heard of who had a doctorate in Shakespearean studies. She was so brilliant, but I was the only one in her class who wasn't bored and didn't throw M&Ms or pennies at her when she read from *Macbeth*. She told me things about myself I'll never forget—the kinds of things that changed my life. Until, finally, she had a nervous breakdown and they took her away. I was there! I saw it! It happened on this one day when she was reading a sensitive Shakespearean sonnet, and the M&Ms and pennies were bouncing off her head—BOING! BOING! Until she couldn't stand it any longer. Suddenly, she opened a classroom window and leaped up onto the ledge! Three stories high above a cement handball court! And she said to the class, "If you don't stop it. I'm going to jump!" That was the first time I learned how much kids like action and suspense, because everyone except me yelled, "JUMP!" But the Dean of Boys ran in and pulled her off the ledge in time. I really miss her. Miss Burger would even let me stay after school and show her my stories. I'd perform them for her with puppets and marionettes. She'd just sit there smiling at me, encouraging me. I even told her a story in which I had invented the perfect sleeping room—a room that was painted all black with just a mattress—and a boy has fantastical dreams of heaven and death. Miss Burger suggested I shouldn't write too many stories about God and death because she said that usually means a writer is finished. But she said she was certain I had nothing to worry about—that I was filled with Life! Filled! That I had *amulets*! There were amulets, magic shields, in my stories to protect me from demons! That I'd always find a way out! I'd escape! I'd win! She was the only one to tell me I wasn't completely deranged! I was just going to be a writer!

Bibliography

Books for Young Adults

1968	*The Pigman*
1969	*My Darling, My Hamburger*
1970	*I Never Loved Your Mind*
1976	*Pardon Me, You're Stepping on My Eyeball*
1977	*Confessions of a Teenage Baboon*
1978	*The Undertaker's Gone Bananas*

1980	*A Star for the Latecomer* (with Bonnie Zindel)
1980	*The Pigman's Legacy*
1981	*The Girl Who Wanted a Boy*
1982	*To Take a Dare* (with Crescent Dragonwagon)
1984	*Harry and Hortense at Harmone High*
1987	*The Amazing and Death-Defying Diary of Eugene Dingman*
1989	*A Begonia for Miss Applebaum*

Plays

1970	*The Effect of Gamma Rays on Man-in-the-Moon Marigolds*
1970	*Let Me Hear You Whisper*
1971	*And Miss Reardon Drinks a Little*
1972	*The Secret Affairs of Mildred Wild*
1975	*Ladies of the Alamo*
1989	*Amulets Against the Dragon Forces*

Movie and TV Scripts (selected)

1972	*Up the Sandbox*
1973	*Mame*
1984	*Maria's Lovers*
1985	*Runaway Train*
1985	*Alice in Wonderland/Through the Looking-Glass*
1986	*Babes in Toyland*
1989	*LET ME HEAR YOU WHISPER* (remake)
1990	*A Connecticut Yankee in King Arthur's Court*

Editor

Donald R. Gallo is professor of English at Central Connecticut State University, where he supervises student teachers and teaches courses in composition and in literature for young adults. In addition to reading widely in the field of books for teenagers, Dr. Gallo became personally acquainted with a number of authors of young adult novels at conferences of the Assembly on Literature for Adolescents of NCTE (ALAN), an organization of which he served as president in 1986–87. Gallo's acquaintances with authors developed further as he solicited, compiled, and edited original short works of fiction by outstanding authors of young adult books for three short story anthologies: *Sixteen, Visions,* and *Connections.* Currently, he is compiling a collection of short plays for young adults written for the occasion by well-known YA authors.